Am I Beautiful?

T0352710

'Chine McDonald offers personal and theological reflections on physical beauty. She challenges the narrow idea we are fed from billboards and magazines, and sketches out a better way to appreciate our own and others' beauty in a diverse, multicultural society. Her thoughtful and vulnerable writing draws the reader from page to page.'

Revd Maggi Dawn – professor of theology and principal of St Mary's College, Durham

'In a style as captivating as her personality, Chine writes about her own struggles with weight, height, hair and colour, with an honesty so real it hurts. This is a liberating must-read for every woman of every size, age, belief and background. Buy it for yourself, your sister, your mother, and most of all, your daughters and granddaughters.'

Michele Guinness – journalist and writer

'It takes courage to answer the question of *Am I Beautiful?* It takes even more vulnerability to stare into the mirror and write where true beauty comes from – within. I applaud Chine and her courage to lift the spirits, hearts and faces of women who feel broken, ugly and ashamed.'

Renee Fisher – the Devotional Diva® and author of Not Another Dating Book; Forgiving Others, Forgiving Me; *and* Loves Me Not.

'Wow – this book is amazing! Hilarious, intimate and wise, it gripped me, not just because as social commentary-cum-confession it's so well-observed, but because the writing is deliriously alive.'

Jenny Taylor – Founder CEO of the London-based Centre for Religious Literacy in World Affairs (Lapido Media) and author of A Wild Constraint: the Case for Chastity

'Being a father to two teenage daughters, I am crushingly aware of the huge pressure they are placed under to conform to society's view of what is beautiful. I can't commend Chine's book highly enough. I for one breathed a sigh of relief that someone was brave enough to start this conversation and that at last there was a resource I could give to my daughters.'

Carl Beech – Christian Vision for Men

'Chine shares her battles with identity and her quest for beauty with unflinching honesty, giving us permission to finally admit our own. *Am I Beautiful?* is raw and powerful, yet inspirational and hopeful. I love this book, and believe it's essential reading for Christian women today.'

Jo Saxton – speaker and author

'Chine is a remarkable woman and this book will help you remember you are beautiful when you feel ugly, lovely when you feel dowdy and cherished when you feel like nothing special.'

Rachel Gardner – founder of Romance Academy and author of Cherished

'I sat down to read this beautiful book literally five minutes after being told by a stranger that I look fatter in my profile picture than I do in real life. It was looking like being a bad day. Until, that is, I got absorbed by this book and was taken on a journey of exploration that made me question why a stranger's comment should spoil my day. Chine approaches the concept of beauty and how we feel about it with grace and vulnerability. This book is more than a biblical exposé on beauty; it's an invitation to step into Chine's story, to walk with her as she reflects on her journey of self-esteem and self-image and to share what she, and her friends, have learned along the way.

This book has the power to transform the way we perceive ourselves, each other and beauty itself. Every woman should read it, every woman should talk about it with her friends and her daughters, because if we can grasp hold of the truths within it, we can shift a culture which continually tells us that we are not beautiful enough.'

Bekah Legg – CEO of Restored

We hear that we are made in the image of God, that he looks at the heart not the outward appearance, that we have been set free from negative thought patterns. But all of this flies out of the window when we look in the mirror and compare ourselves to the images of beauty we are bombarded with both in the media and in everyday life.

We succumb to the beauty myth and beat ourselves up when we fall short of its arbitrary standards, causing ourselves and other women so much pain.

Our story as Christian women really needs to be better than this. Because beauty is only part of the story.

This book calls on women to reclaim our body image, pick up our self-esteem and recognize our true value, leaving us free to be the culture-making, injustice-fighting, Christ-reflecting women we were created to be.

Am I Beautiful?

Breaking free from society's toxic obsession with body image

by Chine McDonald

Authentic

First published 2013 by Authentic Media Limited
PO Box 6326, Bletchley, Milton Keynes, MK1 9GG
authenticmedia.co.uk

Second edition published 2022

British Library Cataloguing in Publication Data
A catalogue record for this book is available from the British Library
ISBN 978-1-78893-292-9
978-1-78893-293-6 (e-book)

Cover Design by Mercedes Piñera

Contents

✳

Foreword

When I was 15, I lost the skin off my face and feet because of severe eczema. I gained 100 pounds from the medication I took to heal my skin rash. Six years later, when I thought my eczema – and severe anxiety – had cleared, I moved states to go to school. And I lost the skin off my hands. I had to go through the process of taking medication, gaining weight, and withdrawing from school once again. Throughout this painful decade between the ages of 15 and 25, I truly believed I was fat, ugly, and that no man would love me.

Lie.

Lie.

All lies.

But I know the truth now. You see, the truth is, even throughout my 'ugly years', I was beautiful. Maybe not in the eyes of the school mates that I separated myself from. Maybe not in the eyes of the fashion magazines. Maybe not in the eyes of society as a whole. But I was beautiful to the One whose idea Beauty was in the first place.

I know that he made me unique. I know that he allowed me to suffer for a reason. I believe I know, along with Chine – as you'll see in the pages that follow – where true beauty lies.

This book is about more than the age-old cliché 'It's what's on the inside that counts'. Because clichés just don't cut it. As Christian women, we hear them so often that they become meaningless. 'Charm is deceptive,' Proverbs 31 says. 'Beauty is fleeting; but a woman who fears the LORD is to be praised.' But deciphering what this charm is, and on which scale we measure true beauty in a world we often fear more than we fear the Lord, is what we need to do – together; joining together as a sisterhood determined no longer to judge each other by the world's standards but to look to our Creator for our worth.

Some might know me as Devotional Diva. But that doesn't mean that they know me. The real me has faced her fair share of ugly days and struggled through the pain of feeling inadequate. I'm guessing you have too. I shared the pain of my beauty journey with Chine and further on in *Am I Beautiful?* you will read a snippet of that story.

Throughout this book, you'll be struck by Chine's openness and vulnerability. In pouring her heart out and bearing her beauty wounds, she shows us that only through sharing the reality of the pressures we women face, can we together find freedom from shame.

To the woman who is reading this book, I praise you. I celebrate your beauty. I stand in awe of the woman God created. It is my hope that through the pages of *Am I Beautiful?* you will come to see what I see, what God sees, and what Chine has discovered.

You.
Are.
Beautiful.

Renee Fisher, Devotional Diva®

Introduction

I've been a woman all my life. I've grown up in a house full of women, surrounded by my mum and sisters, lots of aunties and many female friends. Beautiful, intelligent, witty women of all shapes and sizes. In school, university, the workplace and in church I'm often taken aback by the vast amount of talent and goodness that there is within womankind. We are over-achievers, homemakers, lawyers and artists, teachers and theologians. We could change the world. But there is something that has increasingly started to bug me – something that could be holding us back from reaching our potential. It's that constant murmur of dissatisfaction; not with the state of the world or the unequal pay gap; nor with the fact that 140 million girls and women around the world are currently living with the consequences of female genital mutilation. It's not the unified cry for justice in all areas of society, nor is it the common zeal of women wanting to make the world better. Instead, it's the susurration of low self-esteem and battered self-image that seems to creep its way into the conversations I hear women having by the coffee machine at work, in mums and toddlers groups up and down the country and, most worryingly, in our church pews. I hear it in the swapping of diet tips and the compliments about outfits. I hear it in the conversations about the latest hair-removal techniques and the newest body-controlling underwear. We are constantly looking at our physical bodies and those of the women around us. We are judging each other, subconsciously rating other members of the sisterhood as hot or not – ourselves included. As women, we can be desperately unhappy with our bodies, seeing only our lumps and bumps – whether they are there or not – our cellulite or flat chests. We are constantly dieting. Some of us to extreme lengths that leave us fighting for our lives. Some of us go under the knife because we want to look a little bit more like someone else – someone we perceive has a better nose, smoother skin or fewer wobbly bits.

I'm going to let you into a secret. Some days I feel pretty ugly. Yes, there are some days when I wake up, take a look in the mirror and think that God did an alright job when he made me. I like my eyes. A touch of eyeliner and mascara makes them pop. I have high cheekbones – a family trait for which I'm thankful – that my mother passed on to me and my sisters. It's on these days that I like my 'curvy' figure. I'm thankful for not being flat-chested. On these days, the wardrobe choice seems to make itself and I slip effortlessly into an outfit that makes me feel confident and ready for the day. It's on these sunny days that I can actually believe that in some way I reflect the beauty of God.

> As women, we can be desperately unhappy with our bodies, seeing only our lumps and bumps.

There are *some* days like this.

But, if I'm honest, most days aren't like this at all. At times I feel very un-pretty. I resent the fact that my body must be a product of the Fall – a constant reminder that we don't live in a perfect world. I roll out of bed and can't bear to catch a glimpse of myself in the mirror. I have beady black eyes and my cheeks are puffy – exaggerated like a cartoon character. Even if I do venture towards the mirror – because I have to put my make-up on, to somehow address the mess that's in front of me – I can't bear to look down at the shape of my body. My thighs rub together and I desperately try to find an outfit that in some way will hide my flabby belly. On the Tube I feel like a giant, towering above the petite blonde with the tiny waist who looks like she just stepped out of *Vogue*.

I'm not the only woman who feels this way. When we look in the mirror, as many as 8 out of 10 of us are not happy with the reflection peering back at us – and more than half of us will be seeing something that is not a true reflection of what we look like.[1] Eve was really lucky in the Garden of Eden as she had no one to compare herself to. We, as twenty-first-century women, are not so lucky. The advertising, media and entertainment industries bombard us with images of an ideal towards which we strive, relentlessly banging against the treadmill as that ideal moves further and further away from us and becomes less and less achievable. As a result, many of us are living with this constant feeling that we have failed; that we are inadequate and undesirable. This can affect not just what we see in the mirror but how we relate to the outside world.

I think our story as Christian women really needs to be better than this. We have heard that we are made in the image of the God, in whom the essence of beauty is found. We know somewhere in the back of our minds that God looks at the inside and not at the outer appearance. But yet these truths somehow melt away during the course of everyday life; the times when we can't see past our love handles; the times when we spend such vast amounts of money on our hair, make-up and clothes. These truths are drowned out by the messages we read in magazines and the images we see on our television screens.

We need to fight back against these negative messages and learn again to listen to that still, small voice that whispers to us that we are beautiful because we were created by Beauty itself. We need to remind ourselves of what true beauty is. We must teach ourselves to find value in our identity in Christ and not in the compliments we receive about our physical appearance or when we compare ourselves to anyone else. Because we have to regain the confidence to be bold in going for the goal that God has set before us. Together, as sisters in Christ, we need to be honest about our struggles and then build one another up so that none of us has to suffer in silence because of a shattered self-image.

My Journey

Writing this book has taken me on a journey. But there have been moments on the journey when I've felt like giving up. At times I have felt like packing it all in, closing my laptop and resigning the thousands of words I have written to the trash bin, never to be read again. Because recently I have been so overwhelmed by the brokenness that exists in the world around me. I've learnt of tragedies where children are slaughtered. I witness friends going through heartbreak, sickness, death and disappointment. I see people living not too far away from me who cannot afford to feed their families.

> We need to remind ourselves of what true beauty is.

And me? I'm engrossed in the seemingly trivial question: *Am I beautiful?* Suddenly, all the words I have been writing, the questions I've been asking, the pre-occupation with beauty I've had over the past months seem pointless, worthless, self-indulgent and superficial. Because throughout, I have had this sense of whether – in the grand scheme of life, with its ups and downs, its tragedies, its profound experiences, its wars, its conflict, its injustice and inequality – beauty matters. I see so much hurt and pain going on around me. I see so much wrong with the church and the world in which I live. I want to scream and shout and stomp my feet about the *really* important things. And I've been asking God why I'm writing this. Why I couldn't write about something that would change the world.

And then I stop. And I realize that this *could* change the world. Because beauty is only part of this story. Beauty is actually to do with a much bigger story about the nature of God, our relationship with him, our identity and freedom and value and self-worth. Issues of beauty, self-confidence, body image, and the feelings of inadequacy that can so often surround these issues, are ones that play some part to a lesser or a greater degree in every woman's life. For some, it is a hurt that they live with every single day of their lives. For others, it comes and goes. Some make a conscious effort to not let it take hold of their lives. For others, that feeling of being un-beautiful is crippling. It stops them from fulfilling their potential. It makes them count themselves out. It makes them feel less than anyone else and unable to do what they should be doing.

> Beauty is only part of this story.

You will see throughout this book that so many women suffer from an inherent sense of shame and inadequacy. We are more likely to doubt our own abilities than men are. We are less likely to lead nations, to be at the forefront of culture-shaping organizations. Because so often we feel that we can't. That we are not. That we are incapable. For so many of us, our insecurities are a familiar friend and our worst enemy.

Each time I sheepishly told someone I was writing a book about beauty, I immediately felt vulnerable, insecure and scrutinized. When I told people the title was *Am I Beautiful?* some of them would feel the need to respond with an emphatic 'yes, of course you are!'. Others did that thing where they gave me the once over as if they were rating me in their heads and politely choosing not to answer, taking it as a rhetorical question. I've felt the need to defend myself and over-emphasize the fact that the *I* in *Am I Beautiful?* of course does not refer to *me* but to womankind as a whole. It means that I myself am not being put under the microscope, standing vulnerably in the spotlight. It means that people are not judging me on whatever standard of beauty it is that they choose to measure me by. If I distance myself then it also means I am not being self-indulgent, that I am not looking for validation, begging for people to tell me I'm beautiful. And it means that I am not vain or frivolous, obsessed with beauty when there are children dying in the world. As a journalist, I have been more comfortable with holding up a mirror to society than looking in the mirror myself.

Finding Freedom for a Purpose

When we as women take a deep breath, face the mirror and find security rather than condemnation, we can also find freedom, value and worth. Not so that we can sit around and look at our pretty selves, but so that we can become better equipped to be world-changers. This is why we need to know that we are valuable and loved, that we are of worth, that we are good. The world needs us to believe that we are *beautiful*. And – eventually – we must stop craving it unhealthily, or feeling the need to ask the question. Because when we are secure in our bodies and our identities, we take our eyes off ourselves. We stop looking down at our feet, ashamed and wanting to hide away from the world, hoping that no one will notice us; and we look up – our heads held high, our eyes really seeing the world around us, looking for what it is that needs making whole.

> The world needs us to believe that we are beautiful.

Seeking how we can bring a little bit of the Kingdom of God to our churches, our homes, our workplaces, our schools, our communities, our world.

When we stop craving those things that help to boost our self-esteem we stop relying on the affirmation of others to make us feel good. We are free to find our worth and our affirmation only in God. The words that crowd our heads – that tell us we are ugly, too fat, too skinny, too hairy, too wobbly – are silenced. Because when there is a silence, our hearts and our ears can be open to hearing from God. He tells us that we are wonderfully and beautifully made. And we can hear from him what it is he would have our wonderfully and beautifully created selves do to fulfil the purpose that he has for us.

The world is too broken for us to be preoccupied with feeling ugly. And life is too short not to feel beautiful.

Beyond Pretty

So to the rest of the book. At times in the pages that follow, I'll share some deeply personal stories about my own body struggles and insecurities. Along the way, we'll also hear stories from other women – some well known and some just like you and me – who are on a journey towards finding their worth and value in Christ alone, rather than in their outward appearance.

I hope that as you read this book you'll be inspired to be confident in the person God's made you to be, to challenge the wrong attitudes that subject so many of us to low self-esteem in our world and in our churches, and most of all to feel beautiful – lumps, bumps and all. My prayer is that we will be freed from the chains that make us feel worthless, *less than*, un-beautiful. I long for us to feel released enough to open up about our anxieties, to embrace our vulnerabilities so that we no longer suffer alone but instead throw arms around each other and walk out of this together. But most of all I pray that we might turn our hearts towards the one who sets us free; that we might stop presenting to him the prettiest version of ourselves. God alone sees us in our weakest moments – those times when we raid the fridge in the middle of the night, hungrily gorging ourselves to fill that emptiness that seems unable to ever be filled. He alone sees us when we cower silently over the toilet basin desperately trying to rid our bodies of the bad stuff, in our effort to be sinless, perfect, beautiful. He alone sees us in these our ugliest moments. And he alone still calls us beautiful.

> God alone sees us in our weakest moments.

1.

Craving Beauty

Am I beautiful? We want the answer to be yes. We crave that which is beautiful and we long for it to be true of ourselves. We want to see beauty when we look in the mirror. So we are forever on that journey towards striving to become beautiful – that is valued, of worth, good – because we do not allow ourselves to dare to believe for a moment that we already are.

'A thing of beauty is a joy forever.' (John Keats, Endymion)

'To love beauty is to see light.' (Victor Hugo)

'Dark am I, yet lovely.' (Song of Songs 1:5)

Revelation

I remember the moment I became aware of what I looked like. And it wasn't pretty. I was 5 years old, in reception class at primary school in Greenwich, south-east London. My family had moved to England from Nigeria only the year before. Nati, our beautiful, elegant teacher from Madrid, Spain, had asked each of us to draw a picture of ourselves. The years fall away and I'm that child again, busying myself with the self-portrait . . .

I draw the childlike outline: a face, a body, legs. And then I take the yellow pencil and lovingly colour in my long hair. I reach for the blue pencil and draw big eyes, and then add a dash of pink for the lips. Good work, I think, satisfied. But then Jenna, my childhood best friend, leans over. She takes one look at my picture and says three words that hit me: 'That's not you.' A sudden flash of revelation pummels me in the stomach. The picture I'm drawing looks nothing like me. I don't have blonde hair or blue eyes. I don't look like Jenna or Joanne or Louise. I don't have white skin. Mine's brown. My hair isn't light, but the darkest black. My eyes are brown, not sparkly blue. As I sit before the offending portrait, I wonder, am I not pretty like they are? Aren't I beautiful? I look around at the other boys and girls in the class and realize that I'm the only one who looks like me. Immediately I feel alone. Ugly. I feel foolish and embarrassed that I would even think that I am as pretty as everyone else. I'm not as cute as Cinderella, or Aurora in Sleeping Beauty. *They are beautiful. But they bear no resemblance to me. I feel like running. I hadn't known before Jenna pointed it out that I was different. Prior to that moment, my 5-year-old self had felt content, pretty, beautiful; like little girls should do. Until then I had had no concept of being different or inadequate. I hadn't known what ugly felt like. But who said I was? Who told me I was inadequate? Who told me I was ugly?*

Writing now in a coffee shop in multicultural Manchester, where there is such beauty in diversity, I feel so very angry. My eyes are stinging with rage. I want to travel back in time and reach out to my 5-year-old self and hold her in my arms and reassure her that she is so very beautiful. I want to tell her not to listen to those voices that have appeared from nowhere announcing that because she looks different that she is somehow inadequate; that she is somehow not good enough; that she is somehow ugly. Because I know everything that I've seen and learnt in the 23 years since that moment of realization. I know about the images and the people I've compared myself to. I know the words of condemnation that I've internalized from the culture around me. I know that from that moment on I will continue to feel inadequate. I know the gruelling regimes, the over-eating, the under-eating, the tears while looking in the mirror of changing rooms, the layers and layers of make-up and fake hair that have formed part of my attempt to claim the elusive thing that is beauty for myself.

> We find ourselves constantly falling short.

Yet it turns out that this story of inadequacy and feeling un-pretty belongs not only to me. It's one that seems near universal to woman-kind. We judge ourselves and are judged on how we look in a way that men cannot understand. And because this beauty is our measuring stick, we find ourselves constantly falling short. No matter how beautiful we may actually be.

Shrinking Violet

For me, like for so many women, the feelings of not measuring up in the beauty stakes started when I was a young girl. One of my favourite books growing up as a child was Judy Blume's *Are You There God? It's Me, Margaret*. My friends and I were Blume devotees, devouring every page of her pre-teen books, which seemed to speak of the angst we were experiencing. She totally got us.

As our heroine Margaret pours out to God her sometimes hilarious anxieties about adolescence, she describes her first day at a new school in which the woman she at first thinks is the class teacher actually turns out to be a giant girl who is actually the same age as her. As I read these words again in a worn copy of the book, I'm filled with the horrifying memories of towering above the other little girls in my class. The girl Margaret is referring to might as well be me. Because I was an abnormally tall child. One of my most mortifying memories was appearing on stage as pretty much the world's tallest munchkin in a school production of *The Wizard of Oz* . . .

I am a munchkin. I trudge awkwardly on the stage in a floral dress made by my mother like Gulliver striding amid the Lilliputians. I am 8 years old, but have already reached the average height of a full-grown human woman. I am taller than Dorothy, the Tin Man, Scarecrow and Lion – the cream of the year 6 acting talent. But I'm supposed to pretend like I'm a small person because I'm in year 3 – and my whole class has been collectively cast as the peculiar-looking little guys. But I am tall. Freakishly so. With every mortifying step along the yellow brick road, my cheeks are growing hotter and hotter. I can hear parents whispering: 'Munchkin? She's no munchkin! She's a giant.'
Munchkin mortified.

I was so very tall for my age. Between the ages of 6 and 10 I kept growing and growing, shooting upwards with no signs of slowing, like Jack's beanstalk. There were times when I thought I would never stop; that I would keep growing and growing until I could pick my parents up and put them in my pocket.

Munchkin mortification aside, let me share with you a few more incidents that made me want the ground to swallow up my abnormally tall body. Once, getting on a bus with my two little sisters, the driver asked me how old my daughters were. I was 10 years old. On my first day of secondary school, like the girl in Judy Blume's book, I was presumed to be a teacher. At this point, I had reached the grand old age of 11. When I was 9 years old in primary school, our teacher had decided to show us how to create maths graphs. My heart sank when she announced that we would be creating a graph based on our class members' weights. My eyes are stinging again as I recall being weighed in front of the whole class, and it being announced that I weighed more than the combined weight of the two smallest class members. Twenty years later and my heart is still racing; I still feel sick at the embarrassment and shame of it all. The effect it has had on my life is huge – I was not to step on a scale again for another sixteen years.

Like I said, I was very tall. At the age of 10, I was around 5 ft 8 in – just two inches shorter than I am now. I am a tall woman, but not freakishly so. At some point everyone started to grow too, and most of the boys that were shorter than me have grown into men that are taller than I am.

Being tall was my mortifying thing. Being short may have been yours. Wearing glasses or braces may have filled you with embarrassment as a child. Maybe you tried desperately to hide your freckles. Or maybe you had sticky-out ears or a large nose. No

> I was trying to make myself smaller, to not draw attention to myself.

matter what it was, we can all remember something about our childhood appearances that we were not happy about. Things we wished we could change. Things that made us feel *un-beautiful* and things that caused us to crave that elusive beauty even more.

For me, the way I felt inside manifested itself in how I behaved and in my mannerisms. I remember my mum constantly reminding me not to stoop. I would hunch my shoulders and always have a slight bend in my knee, because I was trying to take up less space. I would be quiet in class and refuse to put my hand up to answer questions I knew the answers to – because I was trying to make myself smaller, to not draw attention to myself.

The way I feel inside still manifests itself in the way I carry myself. When I feel beautiful – when I catch a glimpse of myself and approve of what I see – I walk tall; my shoulders back and my head tilted upwards. I stride across the floor confidently. Upright. I feel I can do anything. But on my *ugly* days, I feel myself trying to hide again. I sit crouched over, my shoulders stooped and hunched, my arms trying to shield my flabby midriff from sight. I cover myself up. I am insecure and that can-do attitude is nowhere to be seen.

That is why I want the beautiful days to far outnumber the ugly ones. Because I see the potential that we, as the female contingent of the body of Christ, have. And I see how we are held back from fulfilling our purposes in God when we don't see ourselves as beautiful. I see the lack of confidence this brings, I see how we beat ourselves up rather than build each other up. I worry about how we spend our time and efforts pummelling our unruly bodies into submission rather than working tirelessly for justice, mercy and the coming of the Kingdom of God. I see how our pre-occupation with ourselves takes up space where we should be welcoming the stranger and comforting the broken-hearted we see everywhere around us. This is why I pray that we might feel beautiful.

Mirror, Mirror on the Wall

If there is a lesson to be learnt from the popular fairy tale *Snow White and the Seven Dwarves*, it's not the virtues of whistling while you work. At the heart of the story, written by the German protestant brothers Jacob and Wilhelm Grimm in 1812, lies a tale of vanity, jealousy, insecurity and the craving for beauty.

Snow White was never my favourite fairy tale. I was more of a Cinderella kinda girl. But when, as a young girl, I heard the story, or watched the cutesy Disney adaptation, I identified with Snow White, the heroine of the story, of course. But as I read the tale afresh as a grown woman, I find myself recognizing some of the wicked queen's actions. Suddenly they don't seem so alien, so evil. They seem familiar. The queen is described as a 'beautiful woman, but proud and haughty'. And we read that 'she could not bear that anyone else should surpass her in beauty'. Every day – *every* day – she would gaze at her reflection in a wonderful talking mirror. She would probably take a moment to admire herself, to smooth back her hair, maybe peer at her features a little closer. And then she would ask it: 'Looking-glass, looking-glass, on the wall, who in this land is the fairest of all?' In other words: 'Looking-glass, looking-glass, on the wall, *am I beautiful?* And the mirror would, without fail, reply: 'Thou, O Queen, art the fairest of all.' Talk about an ego boost to start the day. She probably started to get comfortable with hearing how beautiful she was every morning. She probably revelled in the fact that her super-talking mirror had scanned the length and breadth of the land and found none prettier. She probably started to feel quite secure in that. Maybe the morning beauty check-in became a mere formality, a habit that made her feel pretty good about herself.

Until . . .

Until one day when her 7-year-old step-daughter, the raven-haired, porcelain-skinned Snow White, is judged far more beautiful by the queen's trusty companion, the talking mirror.

Ouch.

'Then the Queen was shocked, and turned yellow and green with envy. From that hour, whenever she looked at Snow White, her heart heaved in her breast, she hated the girl so much.'

This harmless girl then becomes the object of all of the queen's scorn. Her insecurities about the way she looks manifest themselves in ugliness and evil. She orders a huntsman to kill Snow White and bring her heart back as a token. From beauty to ugliness via a mirror.

The story reminds me of another famous one about comparison – the story of Saul and David in the Bible. In 1 Samuel, we hear that Saul – the first king of Israel – really looks the part. We hear that he stands a head taller than other men, that he is extremely handsome, that in every regard he is without equal. If you were going to cast a man in the role of 'king', then you would cast a man like Saul. But later on in the story, young David enters the scene – the man who would be king. He kills the giant Philistine Goliath and becomes the people's champion. So Saul starts to realize that he is losing control. He seems no longer able to keep a lid on his insecurities. And then he comes across a group of women: 'As they danced, they sang: "Saul has slain his thousands, and David his tens of thousands"' (1 Sam. 18:7). How gutting must that have been for Saul? Talk about a punch in the stomach. He had found himself being compared to another, and realized that he had come up lacking. Even though he had slain *thousands*, this seemingly great achievement was trumped by David's tens of thousands. And just like the wicked queen in the story of Snow White: coming second, being judged *less than* another person can be enough to drive you to murder. Both the wicked queen and Saul display fears and insecurities that I see in myself. They seek to have their worth validated in external, arbitrary realities. They, like me, seek affirmation in worldly things – looking-glasses and huddles of women. They ask am I strong, am I brave, am I worthy, am I valuable, am I beautiful?

But there's a reminder in 1 Samuel 16:7 that these things are not what really counts. Because God says to Samuel: 'Do not consider his appearance or his height . . . The LORD does not look at the things people look at. People look at the outward appearance, but the LORD looks at the heart.' When we crave physical beauty or any other physical attribute that people view as positive, we are going after the wrong things. Instead of cultivating inner beauty and strength and character we are going for the outward things, which are temporal and mean little to God.

Mirror Image

Nati, my first school teacher, was unconventional. She loved to tell us stories of ancient myths and long-forgotten morality tales. I remember sitting with the rest of the class on the floor at her feet, wide-eyed, listening to the stories. Like that of Coppelia, the doll so lifelike that she won the heart of a local swain; or the Greek myth of Persephone, the goddess of the underworld. And Narcissus. In the Greek tale, Narcissus was a vain hunter from Thespiae who was known for his beauty. His pride angered the goddess Nemesis who punished those who were arrogant and filled with hubris. One day she lured Narcissus to a pool of water where he glimpsed his own reflection, became enamoured with it and remained there until he died. He had fallen in love with his own reflection and found himself transfixed and unable to depart from it. A life spent staring at your own reflection, totally absorbed in yourself, is no life at all. Because when you're staring at yourself, asking yourself every second of every day whether you are beautiful or not, desperately craving your own beauty, you can't see what else is happening around you. You are forever judging yourself, rating yourself as to whether you are good enough, whether you meet some standard of beauty. When the answer is yes, when your reflection tells you that you are indeed beautiful, it can momentarily feed an inner craving – fill an emptiness that you are longing to fill. Momentarily. Until that feeling runs out and you are left once again empty. And when your reflection tells you that you are *less than*, that you are not enough, it leaves you, again, empty.

On my pretty days, I am more like Narcissus than I would like to be. But for me, personally, my mirror obsession only applies to looking at my face. For the rest of my body, it's a whole different story. Do you ever look at your body? I mean *really* look? I'm happy to look at my face. I can stand right against the mirror with my nose pressed against it and am content with what I see – as long as I have my make-up on. But it's a totally different story when it comes to the rest of me. When I look at myself in a full-length mirror I do this strange squinty thing as if trying to create my very own magic eye illusion. I stand as far back from the mirror as I possibly can. And I look, only letting my eyes rest on the rough outline of my shape. And this shape isn't my real shape because I suck my tummy in and almost stand on tiptoes in an unnatural stance to make my thighs look longer and thinner. And I tend to look at myself sideways. Facing myself full-on would be too much of an ordeal. I'm not sure why I ever look in the mirror in the first place. When I do, I'm wearing underwear at the very least. Because I long so much to be seen as beautiful, I avoid looking at the parts of me that I feel will betray me. So, for that reason, I am afraid of facing the reality that I know I will be presented with when I look in the mirror.

So I have never looked at myself naked.

I've never looked at myself. Naked.

I have never seen myself naked.

I have never looked at myself.

> 'Adam and his wife were both naked, and they felt no shame.'
>
> (Gen. 2:25)

Shall I tell you why I can't look at myself? Because, quite frankly, I feel ashamed. I fear that when I look at my body – *really* look – that I'll see all the wrong choices that I've made. I'll see that I'm inadequate. I'll see that underneath it all, away from other people, I'm a mess. My clothes – the things I put on to present a together picture to the outside world – are just a cover-up. I'm a fraud. If only everyone knew what lies beneath. If only they saw the stretch marks and the hair in the wrong places and the flabby bits. That's why I haven't looked at myself stark naked in the mirror. I'm afraid and ashamed. Even to stand in front of myself. I'm like Adam and Eve after the Fall, cowering and covering themselves up to shield themselves from God in the Garden of Eden. The God who had created them. The God who had formed Adam out of the dust of the earth and lovingly created Eve out of his rib. The one who knew them better than they knew themselves, and even knew what they had become. He's the one they were hiding from. He's the one they couldn't bear to be naked in front of.

I was challenged when I came across one woman's story detailing her complex relationship with her reflection. In March 2011, Kjerstin Gruys took on a brave challenge – a year-long mirror fast. Allowing herself a one-month transitional period in which she learnt how to apply make-up mirror-less, and put in her contact lenses, she took up the challenge six months before her wedding. That meant she had no idea what she looked like on her wedding day; she did not see herself in her wedding dress. She was also not allowed to look at photos of herself taken throughout the course of the year. For twelve months she did not see herself. She did, however, allow herself the luxury of looking at her shadow. Kjerstin, 29, who had previously suffered from an eating disorder and worked in the fashion industry, undertook the mirror fast when she felt her previous insecurities returning. She found that her mirror fast helped her to start seeing her self-esteem as separate from how she looked, or how she perceived the way she looked. New York beauty writer Autumn Whitefield-Madrano, 36, also went on a similar mirror fast for a month. 'I was surprised at how quickly I stopped worrying about how I looked,' she wrote. 'And if I wasn't thinking about it, I assumed no one else was either, which is actually true.' She also realized that the mirror only confirms what we know is there. The vast majority of the time it does not present us with any new information.

Studies have been done that show that on average women look in the mirror up to 70 times a day, which means we spend a full five days a year gazing at ourselves. Around half wouldn't leave the house without looking in the mirror first. We look and we look and we look, searching and searching and searching. And longing. And longing. And longing. Craving beauty; and craving some satisfaction. But we just can't get any. We are desperately looking for acceptance and validity. But we can't find it in our reflection. This search for acceptance and validity in the mirror is something that starts in our earliest years. And, according to psychologist Dr Vivian Diller, our love-hate relationship with the mirror reflects the ambivalent relationship we have with our bodies. 'Our first mirrors are the reflections we see in our parents' eyes when we are infants,' she writes. 'The gleam – or lack of one – in our parents' gaze begins to shape how we view ourselves.'[2]

> On average women look in the mirror up to 70 times a day.

My Reflection

I am the wicked queen and Narcissus and Kjerstin Gruys. I revel in the times when, feeding my inner craving to be beautiful, my looking-glass tells me that I am just that. Beautiful. But when it tells me that I'm nowhere near the fairest in the land, I am crushed. On those days when the mirror is kind to me, I gaze at it a little too long. I pout and open my eyes wide, or adopt a sultry mirror face that I would probably receive worried looks about if I were to take it out in public.

Dr Phillippa Diedrichs, a psychologist at the Centre for Appearance Research in Bristol, has said that fads such as mirror fasting are actually another form of obsession about our appearance. Instead of staying away from the mirror, she encourages those with issues about their bodies to adopt a 'mirror exposure technique'. They are encouraged to really look at themselves rather than hide away. And instead of criticizing their bodies, try accepting them – fully. So today I did just that. For the first time ever, I took a long, hard look at my body. Without any adornment. Just me. Just as I am. I held my breath. And I opened my eyes to look at me. I resisted the urge to be ashamed and to cover myself up. And I quietened the voices that said: 'if only you could change that bit'. And for a little while I just stood in front of myself, looking. I'm not sure what I had expected. Having never done it before, I was genuinely afraid of what I would see. For weeks, I had been psyching myself up for this act, which for so many women is a totally normal part of their daily routine. When I looked at myself there were no surprises. Because deep down, I know what my body looks like. I know who I am. Realizing that set me free of something – something that I had been avoiding facing for a long time; the realization that, although I may not be perfect, I am beautiful – just as I am.

Christ Focus

Kjerstin Gruys first decided to undertake a mirror fast after reading a story about an order of nuns living centuries ago who vowed never to look at their own bodies. The passage in *The Birth of Venus* describes how the nuns focused on the cross when they bathed or changed their clothes, rather than looking at themselves. Kjerstin, inspired by these mirror-free nuns, thought the idea sounded freeing rather than restricting.

And that's just it. Our focus, in all things, must be on the cross, on Christ our Saviour. It's only in him that we see a clear, true reflection of ourselves. Not tainted by society's images of bodies. Not in comparison to others' beauty. Not wracked by guilt, or spoilt by arrogance. The mirrors we are looking through today, on this earth – the ones we obsess over – are murky and distorted. It's amazing to think that the Bible talks about mirrors and tells us that the mirror is not the truth that we should set our eyes on. I read in 1 Corinthians 13:12 that: 'For now we see only a reflection as in a mirror.' But it continues that then – *then* – 'we shall see face to face'. I love *The Message* translation of this verse: 'We don't yet see things clearly. We're squinting in a fog, peering through a mist. But it won't be long before the weather clears and the sun shines bright! We'll see it all then, see it all as clearly as God sees us, knowing him directly just as he knows us!'

> I long for that day when we will see ourselves clearly.

I long for that day when we will see ourselves clearly. I can't wait for that day when, given the opportunity at last to really see ourselves, we will glimpse the perfect picture of ourselves in relation to God; to truly see ourselves the way he sees us. No longer craving, but knowing that we are nothing without him and everything in him. I resonate with what the executive director of Mercy Ministries UK says about how a distorted mirror can ruin women's lives. Arianna Walker's work supports young women with life-controlling issues such as eating disorders, self-harm and depression. She says: 'God's mirror, his word, will tell us exactly what we are worth and how loved we are. Its reflection is clear, unchanging and not dependent on whether we think we deserve it or not. God's word is very clear about our beauty, our value and our worth.'[3] I hear her words and know that they are truth. I know that I know these things. I've heard all this before. But I wonder why these eternal truths seem so easy to forget when I look in the mirror. Once again, the Bible provides insight here. James 1:23–24 says: 'Anyone who listens to the word but does not do what it says is like someone who looks at his face in a mirror and, after looking at himself, goes away and immediately forgets what he looks like.' So often, we are fed with the truth of the word of God and what it says about our identity in Christ. But just as quickly we forget and become hungry again. Once again we find ourselves craving beauty.

I wonder whether we can ever expect to be fully satisfied in our beauty, or whether, as so often seems to be the case with the Christian life, we will continually oscillate between overflowing and empty, between feeling beautiful and feeling ugly, between wholeness and brokenness, between satiated and craving. Maybe we'll only be permanently satisfied in our own beauty once we get to eternity. But it is so easy to fall into the trap of thinking we'll be 'fixed' in the afterlife and that for now we must succumb to the faulty realities of our earthly selves. So often when the Bible talks about the Kingdom of God, it talks about that which is to come. But at other times it suggests that the Kingdom of God starts now. So the same goes for the way we see ourselves. We won't just see ourselves as God sees us when we leave this earth. It's a process that begins today. Because we have been saved by grace, we have been brought into relationship with our Creator God. And because we're in perfect communion with him, the mirror becomes less murky, we can see the true picture of ourselves and we can be satisfied in it – starting now.

If a Tree Falls

There is a famous metaphysical question posed in the 1920 book *Physics* by Charles Riborg Mann and George Ransom Twiss, which asks: 'When a tree falls in a lonely forest, and no animal is nearby to hear it, does it make a sound?' Why? It is an attempt to understand the nature of knowledge and what makes things true and real.

Well, I have another question for you. If no one could ever see you, would you care what you look like? It's a question I've been mulling over recently. When we ask whether we are beautiful, are we talking about whether we are beautiful in and of ourselves; whether we are full of beauty; or are we asking whether other people think we're beautiful? Whichever way you answer that question, it tells you something about what it means for you to be beautiful, or to believe that you are so.

> We don't feel we are beautiful in our natural state.

As for me, I care at least a little bit less about what I look like if no one is going to see me. It's as if my craving is to be considered beautiful by others, rather than be beautiful in and of itself. If I get one of those precious days when there's nothing in the diary so I can just lay out on the couch watching DVDs and reading books, then I really do not care what I look like. In fact you might be somewhat alarmed if you were to catch me on one of these days. I look an absolute mess. But I feel totally relaxed, totally myself. I let my guard down. It also means that I don't have to put on a front. Because it's just me, myself and I. I am the only person I would dare let see me in this state. I am the only person I feel comfortable enough with to be the real me – warts and all.

Have you ever had one of those awkward moments when you're in this totally relaxed state – you're wearing slacks and a T-shirt? You haven't brushed your hair yet. Maybe you haven't even brushed your teeth! But yet you're totally not bothered. And then there's a knock at the door. Oh dear. You have a decision to make. Do you open the door and let somebody – whether the postman or your neighbour – see you looking a hot mess? Or do you lie still on the couch, not making a sound, hoping that they will go away and come back when you're looking more 'yourself'. I confess I have chosen the second option on a couple of occasions. I wouldn't dare think you have ever done the same, but just in case you have – what does this say about us? Well, it tells us that we don't feel we are beautiful in our natural state – without the make-up and the hairdos and the control pants and the great outfits. It tells us that we try to present to other people a more 'beautiful' version of ourselves than our natural state. It tells us that we really do care what people think about what we look like.

Today I posted my question on my Twitter and Facebook profiles – and the responses were telling. The answers got me thinking a bit more about who we are being beautiful for. But they also showed me that we, too, have become used to seeing the most perfect versions of ourselves when we look in the mirror.

Here are some of the answers people gave me to the question 'if no one could see you, would you care what you look like?':

'Can I see myself? If so, yes.'

'Yes, I love wearing make-up even if it's just for me!'

'If no one saw me from now on, yes, I would still be bothered. But if from birth, I doubt I would care!'

'Depends if I could also see myself. I exist very happily (perhaps more happily) without a mirror.'

'I don't care now so if no one could see me, I can only imagine what I would look like. Bye bye make-up, bye bye razor!!'

'Yes – so much of it has to do with self-worth. Indicator of depression/illness etc. is lack of personal care including make-up, hair, clothes, etc.'

'How thoroughgoing is your "no one"? Does it include me? Other people's perspectives that I've internalized?'

All these answers seem to suggest that, while our perceptions of ourselves and our own beauty are heavily dependent on our being viewed by our friends, family and society as a whole, we also still ask *ourselves* whether we are beautiful – even if no one else is looking.

Because *we* are looking. There seems to be something within us that so desperately wants to be beautiful – even if no one else can see us. And if we are looking at ourselves through our own eyes, then we have to admit that our eyes are still looking at our bodies through a lens that is coloured by society's perceptions of beauty. Our minds are full of images of what a beautiful woman should look like. Every time I look at myself I am actually comparing myself to all those thousands upon thousands of images that I have seen of beautiful women throughout my life. Even if we say that we would still care if we were the only people viewing ourselves, our *selves* have internalized the way that society looks at women. We all have pictures of ourselves that we really like – those are the ones we upload as our Facebook profile photographs. And we all have photos of ourselves that we hate – the ones we delete and forever banish to the recycling bin. This means that there are some images of ourselves that we deem closer to the ideal that is 'beauty' and some that are further away. And that is with our own eyes being the judge and jury. But even our eyes are tainted. But there's more. One friend said that even if no one is looking, taking care of yourself and taking part in a bit of personal grooming are all part of valuing ourselves. Our beauty is tied up in our sense of self-worth.

We all have friends who go through hard times. And for some women the hard times manifest themselves in them no longer taking care of their physical bodies – their inner craving for beauty is broken somehow, or is ignored. They come in to work or church looking dishevelled, hair unkempt and without the make-up that they normally wear. When we think little of ourselves we no longer think it's important to make ourselves look the best we can be. Earlier this year I bought a brand new flat. When I got the keys, I walked into it and – although it was the culmination of months of forms and financial organizing and prayer – it felt empty. It looked like a box to me. It looked like it had not yet got its character. It had not yet found someone to look after it. So as soon as I moved in, I set about decorating it, giving it colour and character – making it look something like a home that somebody lived in and which somebody loved. When people visit my home, I love them to tell me how great it looks. I love the compliments that it receives. Because I love it and I value it. It is an extension of myself. It is an outward display of the person that I am. And I want people to think it's beautiful. If I were to let it fall into disrepair, it would be because I no longer valued it. I no longer cared what people thought of it. It would mean that I no longer loved it. I hope I never fall out of love with my flat. And I pray that, in the same way, I will value my body; that I will treasure it and that I will want it to be all it can be.

Made to Crave

There is something deep within me that craves that which is beautiful. I both want to see beauty and I want to be beauty. I want to align myself with it. This beauty that I crave, however, is not just physical beauty. It's about far more than me desperately wanting to be hot. It's like when you have a craving for some kind of food, but you don't quite know what it is. So you taste and you taste and you taste, never quite finding the satisfying bite that hits the spot. Nothing is quite right, although it might feel like it is

> He is the source of all goodness and truth.

for a moment. I think the thing we are craving when we long for beauty – long to see it, to be it, to taste it – is God. We'll explore in the next chapter how true beauty is merely a reflection of God, who is Beauty itself. The Psalmist beautifully illustrates this inner craving: 'As the deer pants for streams of water, so my soul pants for you, my God. My soul thirsts for God, for the living God' (Ps. 42:1–2). We crave beauty because we crave God. He created us to long for him, to never be satisfied until we are in relationship with him. Love, acceptance, affirmation, belonging and wholeness – all the good things – find their full completion in being in relationship with God.

We have already been brought into relationship with God because of Jesus' sacrifice. It's God's grace that draws us into his embrace. I am beautiful because I'm loved by him, and I'm beautiful because I'm created in his image. What a difference that should make when I look in the mirror; when I constantly search in my reflection for a trace of the beauty of God, which was there all along. So what can we do to satisfy our cravings? Stop looking in the wrong places for fulfilment. Instead, taste and see that God is good. That he is the source of all goodness and truth – and that's beautiful.

Prayer

Dear Lord,
Help me to realize that nothing can satisfy me but you. Thank you that I can find complete wholeness, value and worth in you alone. Help me to feel whole and not broken, help me to feel valuable and not worthless, loved and not rejected. Fill that inner craving I have for beauty with . . . you; the source of everything beautiful. Help me to see you as you are and see myself the way you see me: beautiful.
Amen

Questions to Ponder

- What do you see when you look in the mirror?
- When have you felt at your most beautiful? Why?

- What feelings do you experience when someone tells you that you are beautiful?
- Do you believe, like Arianna Walker does, that God's word is clear about our beauty, our value and our worth?
- What are the things that make us forget our true reflection?

Beauty Challenge

Consider going on a twenty-four-hour or seven-day mirror fast. Note down in a journal your feelings about it. Do you feel anxious or liberated?

2.

Defining Beauty

Am I beautiful? What do I mean by 'beautiful'? There is a flavour of the beauty of God that is felt in seeing some of the world's most majestic scenes. And we experience that same essence in a baby's eyes and the beauty of a woman. But our society distorts that beauty, turning it into something arbitrary and artificial, putting pressure on that beautiful woman rather than liberating her.

'At some point in life, the world's beauty becomes enough.
You don't need to photograph, paint or even remember it. It is enough.'
(Toni Morrison, *Tar Baby*)

'Every experience of beauty points to infinity.' (Hans Urs von Balthasar)

'Few of us seem to be aware that the beautiful packs a power not only to fascinate but also to convince a mature and honest mind of solidly grounded truth.' (Thomas Dubay, *The Evidential Power of Beauty*)

Bye-bye Barbie

I remember being ecstatic when my parents bought me my first Barbie doll. All the other little girls had them and I had longed for my own. I remember spending hours with friends playing with our Barbies and being green with envy because more often than not theirs had far more accessories than mine did. Their Barbies' wardrobes seemed to be filled with dazzling, glitzy choices. They seemed to have more pretty things. But I loved my Barbie all the same. She was a symbol of girlhood and innocence. But she was also mysterious, as if her body and her beauty symbolized some knowledge that I was yet to be made aware of. Even at a young age, I seemed to grasp the idea that Barbie was some kind of archetype, a definition, of what women should be: beautiful, glamorous, graceful. Blonde, slim, blue-eyed and curvy. I remember spending ages brushing her hair with that tiny pink brush and smoothing her long, blonde locks with my fingers as her eyes remained fixed in a vacant expression. Mimicking the girls I'd seen brushing their own hair before bed on the TV, I did the same for Barbie. Although Barbie's hair looked and felt how I perceived a beautiful woman's should, I was also very aware that it looked and felt nothing like my own. The effects of this realization on my little-girl self were of course subtle and would have contributed to me feeling that people who looked like me, and not like Barbie, were counted out of the beauty rankings.

I loved Barbie as a child, but now I don't think there is a better example of a man-made perversion of beauty than her. Holding her up as the definition of what is beautiful could be one of the subtle factors contributing to so many young girls' insecurities about their bodies. Think about how Barbie compares to a real woman. Over the years, there has been a lot written about the fact that her vital statistics, shape and dimensions are unrealistic when compared to ours. If Barbie were real, her measurements would be along the lines of 36-18-38. Sheesh.

But this unrealistic body shape is what we have presented to young girls ever since 1959 when she first went on sale, signalling a new pattern in little girls' play behaviour. In that year, 300,000 dolls were sold and it is estimated that over a billion Barbies have been bought since then, in more than 150 countries. Today 90 per cent of girls aged between 3 and 10 own a Barbie.

> Today 90 per cent of girls aged between 3 and 10 own a Barbie.

To be able to truly know that I am beautiful, I have to wake up to the realization that there are standards of beauty that are unrealistic and man-made – like Barbie; that there are standards of beauty that in fact are caricatures that elevate certain arbitrary characteristics and hold them up on a pedestal. If I don't reject these man-made notions of beauty then I'm going to be left constantly feeling ugly, forever jumping to touch the pedestal and always finding that I simply cannot reach.

I guess now, a long time after I have stopped playing with Barbie, I've continued to often count myself out when it comes to beauty. Maybe you have too at times. But for the most part as I grew older, I grew in the understanding that there were beautiful women who didn't look like Barbie. And I started to toy with the idea that I, too, could be a beautiful woman. But there were some setbacks – the main one being a society that often still reveres the unrealistic Barbie-doll beauty standard for women. And a society that seemingly fails to remember that black can also be beautiful. I remember one particular setback on my beauty journey. It was one of those days when everything seemed to fall into place. I was standing in the train carriage on my way into work in London, boldly reading a book about how Jesus liberates women. And I felt free; totally ready to go out and change the world. And then over someone's shoulder I just happened to see a headline printed on a newspaper: 'Black women "least attractive", says study.' When I read the words, a deep sense of shame washed over me. I was mortified. I was the only black woman in that train carriage. And I felt like a failure. I felt angry, alone and – ugly. I later found out the article reported on a study written by psychologist Satoshi Kanazawa of the London School of Economics that was published in a blog post on *Psychology Today*. Kanazawa had posed the question in his research: Why are Black Women Less Physically Attractive Than Other Women? As if this was an accepted understanding – that black women are objectively not as beautiful as those from other races. Global outrage followed the publication of this article and *Psychology Today* decided to take the post down from their website. Commentators and fellow psychologists have since rubbished the findings as scientifically flawed, while many have called the study racist. In the days following the publication of this article, I learnt that I was not the only black woman to find it deeply distressing. Writing on her Facebook wall, one of my friends – an award-winning novelist in her 20s – wrote under a link to Kanazawa's study: 'I know this is stupid, but it makes me want to cry.' Why had such a useless study provoked such a reaction in confident and successful women? Why, though the study had been dismissed as flawed and racist, did it make us cry? Maybe because deep down inside we all crave beauty in physical form. We long for it. We want beauty to be a description

We want beauty to be a description of us.

of us. When we look up the definition of beauty in the dictionary, we want it to include ourselves: beauty = allure, charm, loveliness, me.

For many black women who have grown up in the West, the study reminded us of the feelings of rejection and isolation that had accompanied growing up being the only little girl that was different. Many of us thought ourselves outside the realm of that which is beautiful. So this study felt like a kick in the teeth. It felt as if nothing had changed since the playground, where my experience seemed typical of many young black children. In the famous Clark Doll Experiment of 1954, which took place in Harlem, New York City, black children aged between 6 and 9 were shown a black doll and a white doll and asked to choose between them based on which doll was the 'nicest' and which one they would prefer to play with. The majority chose the white doll. In a re-creation of the study in the mini-film *A Girl Like Me* by Kiri Davis in Harlem in 2005, not much had changed. The black children still chose the white doll, and agreed the black doll 'looked like them' even though they identified it as being the 'bad one'. This feeling that black women are not beautiful is not just found in Western societies either. The number of skin-bleaching products available in Africa has increased significantly in recent years. The World Health Organization reports that 77 per cent of Nigerian women have used these potentially dangerous skin-bleaching products, while 59 per cent of those from Togo have, 35 per cent of South Africans and 25 per cent of Malians. This feeling that we do not fit into a narrow definition of beauty lies deep within a woman's psyche, regardless of her skin colour. Sometimes we look at ourselves and think that we are the 'bad one'. That we are not good and that we are not beautiful; that the description 'beautiful' applies to someone else, despite our craving for it to be used to describe us. With every image, every doll, that we create that leads a little girl to think that she is not OK as she is, we are robbing her of her childhood. We are force-feeding her insecurity when, instead, she should be made to feel secure, at home in her own body. And we are telling her that she is not beautiful.

The Eye of the Beholder

I grew up in a society that suggested that blonde, blue-eyed, long-haired, slim but busty women were the height of beauty. I am – nearly – none of those things. So I grew up feeling that I was not considered beautiful, as far as my society was concerned. But I was still drawn to the beauty that I felt I did not possess; which is why, as a pre-pubescent girl, I had crushes on the likes of Jason Donovan – a blue-eyed blonde who played Scott in Australian soap opera *Neighbours*, and Robbie Williams from the boy band Take That. These were the people whose images – cut out from teen magazines such as *Just Seventeen* and *Smash Hits* – adorned my walls. As I grew older, it was men like Leonardo DiCaprio and Brad Pitt who I giggled over with girls in my class. We all daydreamed about the same men – the same men that little girls up and down the country also daydreamed about. We spurred each other on and whipped ourselves up into frenzies over these pin-ups. These were the men our culture told us we should find attractive, that we should think fitted the description of 'beautiful'. But none of these men looked like me, or like my dad, or my uncles, or cousins. I grew up in a Western culture that not only made me think that I did not fall into the 'beautiful' category, but that made me believe that white skin and blue eyes were the ideal beauty that I should be attracted to. We live in a world that squeezes the ineffable, otherworldly sense of the beauty that comes from God into a culture-shaped container so that you are defined as beautiful if you fit that transient mould.

If your culture projects a certain image of beauty, then that is what you will consider beautiful. Take *The Girl from Ipamena* – the second most recorded track of all time, which has been covered by the likes of singers such as Frank Sinatra. Written by Antonio Carlos Jobim and Vincius de Moraes in 1962, it is an ode to the beauty of a woman; one woman in particular – Helo Pinheiro – a striking 19-year-old brunette who would walk past Velossa cafe in the district of Ipanema in Rio de Janeiro, Brazil. She was a head-turner – eliciting stares and breaking hearts as she strolled down to the beach unaware of just how beautiful she was.

It's a beautiful story and she was, and is, a beautiful woman. But the story behind the song tells us something deeper about how beauty is perceived differently in different cultural contexts. In the original Portuguese version, the writers emphasize her 'sweet swing', the 'girl with the body of gold'. You imagine a South American swing – curvaceous, curved. But in the most famous recording by Sinatra, the lyrics are changed. The line 'tall and tan and young and lovely' is used to represent the cultural difference in what is considered beautiful in North America as opposed to South. Here we see society's influence on our own perceptions of beauty and of ourselves – and how much the environment and the time we are in influences the decisions that we think we have made of our own free will. When I visit Nigeria or the more urban and multi-ethnic environments of London, for example, it feels like I have more of a chance of being described as beautiful, because, in these cultures, it's not the skinny blonde who is beautiful, but people who look a bit more like me. This shows once again that beauty – though in its essence and in its existence is universally acknowledged – is received and described subjectively.

> Beauty is in the eye of the culture beholding it.

Beauty is in the eye of the culture beholding it. It seems that there is some agreement on seemingly arbitrary things, which perhaps highlight some positive aspect of a female's biological make-up. But we just have to look around to know that what is beautiful is not only decided upon by the eye of the beholder, but differs depending on the context in which you live, or have grown up. For example, in the Kayan tribe in Burma and Thailand, long necks are considered beautiful. So for many centuries, girls from the age of 5 have worn brass rings around their necks to elongate them. More rings are added as the girl grows older to achieve what is deemed an elegant swan-like, beautiful neck.

I'm always struck by the irony that the beauty industries in Africa, Asia and South America have shelves upon shelves stacked with skin-lightening creams and appliances, while in Western countries such as the UK and America, white pasty skin is a no-no and people will regularly use fake tan or spend hours at tanning salons to get that bronzed look. In the US, fat camps, where chubby children are sent by their parents to shed some pounds, are oversubscribed. But in Mauritania, daughters are often sent to camps where they are forced to eat up to 16,000 calories a day so that they will become fatter and therefore more beautiful.

We think we know what we mean when we talk about human beauty, and understand what its true definition is. But really we do not. As finite beings, influenced by what we see and the context in which we are in, we find it difficult to have a God's-eye view of beauty. Because the concept of beauty, as far as humanity is concerned, is forever shifting. And we can thank the fashion industry for that.

How Society Distorts Beauty

There are few women that the world deems as beautiful as Leah Darrow. She has featured in *FHM* magazine and was one of the models picked for the third season of *America's Next Top Model* (*ANTM*) – the world's most famous show pitting beautiful women against each other. Finally, by appearing on the show, she had fulfilled one of her lifelong ambitions – to get into the fashion industry. After her time on the show, she worked as a model in New York. But, when she renewed her faith in God, she realized that all that she had hoped the industry would be, turned out to be shallow and empty. I wanted to find out from her what it feels like to be beautiful enough to be a top model.

So when I got the chance to speak to her I came right out and asked her: 'Are you beautiful?' Her answer: 'The world has a very different standard to how God has defined beauty. When we think of beauty,

we automatically think of what the world thinks, what's in the fashion
magazines or the fashion industry. I guess by being chosen to be on
ANTM it showed that the world's standard saw me as pretty enough
to be on this TV show. But this is not the standard of beauty I now
hold to myself. Not at all. In fact, the more and more I come to know
God and my love for him, I see how distorted that is. All that lies
within us that is true, good and beautiful is because we are made in God's
image and reflect his infinite perfection. So, yes, I do see myself as beautiful in that I was made in the image
and likeness of God and that he is the author of beauty. All creatures bear a
certain resemblance to God. We look at snow-capped mountains and deep blue
seas and we say that they're beautiful,

> The beauty industry only cares about the outside and the standards of what they hold as in style this season or next season.

vast and majestic. They're amazing. So if we can see the beauty in a
mountain, think of how much more beautiful we as creatures created
by God are.'

But this was not her thinking when she headed towards the
bright lights of the runway. 'By the time I was on *ANTM* I was
pretty far from my faith. I was definitely more fascinated with the
world of glamour and beauty and money and fame than I was of
being a faithful Christian. This wasn't as exciting as what the world
could offer me. When Tyra Banks would say something was beautiful, I would mimic it. But everything was exterior, I found while
working as a model in New York. The fashion industry doesn't care
at all about who you are as a person or how you're doing or how you
are mentally or spiritually, or how you're developing your character.
The beauty industry only cares about the outside and the standards
of what they hold as in style this season or next season. And if
you're not willing to do this or that, there's a line of girls behind you

willing to lower their values or forget them altogether to do the job. I realized that I was nothing more than a puppet to them. I realized that the only place where we really can find our home is in God, in our creator.'

She came back to faith in 2005 and since then has been studying theology and spreading the gospel in far-off places around the world. 'The more I study the Bible, the more I see how much God loves us. It's in him you find your centre and the basis for all truth, goodness and beauty.' She also quit the modelling industry. 'I decided I would put that to rest. Each one of us makes an impact in the world. And I did not want to have the impact of a fashion model. I wanted to change the world in a positive way that showed God's truth, goodness and beauty. The fashion industry distorts it. I know there are some pockets that do a much better job than others but as a whole that industry distorts the most beautiful and the most true. And I didn't want to be a part of that.'

She has made some drastic changes in her life and completely changed her wardrobe, opting for modest but not drab. She no longer wears bikinis on the beach because she realized that they emphasize nakedness and encourage people to see women as parts rather than their whole. As someone who has never even dared to think of wearing a bikini, I wonder whether this beautiful woman ever has ugly days, if she ever feels un-pretty or *less than*. 'I probably suffered from a body image disorder during my model-

> I thought I wasn't tall enough or skinny enough, or thought maybe I should be blonde or a redhead.

ling years,' she says. 'I would often see my body as not good or not good enough compared to all the other models – whether in the fashion magazines or the ones standing next to me in the photo shoot. I thought I wasn't tall enough or skinny enough, or thought maybe I should be blonde or a redhead. I know now that what lay at the heart of that was a sense of self-doubt; a feeling that I wasn't good enough or worthy enough as who I was. We allow our culture to define who we are, but we forget that God has the answers.'

My jaw drops in disbelief. I mean, how can such a beautiful woman doubt her beauty? 'We all have feelings of self-doubt. I still have my moments when I look in the mirror and am not completely satisfied with what I see. But I have better tools to deal with that now. I know that the devil is the prince of lies. Sometimes when my husband tells me I look beautiful, I tell him I don't *feel* beautiful. And he reminds me that just because I don't feel beautiful, it doesn't mean that I am not beautiful. Feelings have never been given the task of seeking truth. You have to know even if you don't feel that way that God loves you and created you and is thrilled with your beauty. He is so infinitely happy in you. I think that as women today we really should be striving to be beautifully confident or beautifully good or beautifully true. The material elements of beauty mean very little without truth and goodness. There's too much emphasis on lipstick rather than kind words or manicures rather than a helping hand and appearances and status rather than doing the right thing for your neighbour. It goes for me too. I constantly have to keep myself in check.'

Leah tells me of trips to places such as Ghana and the Philippines where she met local women. They touched her skin and her hair and wished that they looked more like her – lighter. 'I remember thinking I had never seen such beautiful women with their beautiful dark skin and beautiful hair. And I realized that all of us, no matter where we are on the planet, struggle to believe that what God has put forth is true.'

Beauty Struggle

So many women struggle with believing that they are beautiful when they exist in a world that more often than not says they are not beautiful enough. In 2011, the global brand Dove revealed the findings of an extensive worldwide study into women's relationship with beauty. *The Real Truth About Beauty: Revisited* formed part of the brand's Campaign for Real Beauty. Here was a company that, realizing that beauty was more often than not a cause for anxiety among women, said enough is enough. Even after years of campaigning, listening to women themselves, holding the beauty industry to account and raising awareness of the issue, their extensive study found that just 4 per cent of women in the world would consider themselves beautiful. Just 4 per cent of women would tick the 'yes, I am beautiful' box even in an anonymous survey. We are more likely than our brothers, boyfriends, husbands and male colleagues to be painfully unhappy with

> Just 4 per cent of women in the world would consider themselves beautiful.

how we look. In fact, men looking in the mirror are much more likely to rate their bodies as more attractive than they are. Research found: 'Some men looking in the mirror may literally not see the flaws in their appearance.'[4] What makes the girls so much less confident than the boys? When women in the survey were posed the question 'Do you think you're beautiful?', nearly all of them said: 'No. I am not beautiful.'

But are we being conditioned to feel un-beautiful, to always crave beauty but be under no illusion that beauty is actually unattainable? Because pop singers tell us that we don't know how stunning we are to them. Handsome stars croon about loving those bits of us that we can't stand. And they love us precisely because we are oblivious to our own beauty. The underlying message here is that we can't be beautiful if we think we are. And that's down to the fact that this standard of beauty, which looms over our heads, is unachievable. For a reason. So that none can boast. But it's not just that we say we aren't good-looking. Despite craving beauty, a lot of women truly find it hard to believe that they are beautiful.

The Guardian newspaper has a column called 'What I see in the mirror', in which well-known people briefly describe what they see when they look at themselves. In August 2011, it was the turn of Andrea Corr, lead singer of Irish band The Corrs, to take a look at herself. She revealed that although she was once voted the most beautiful woman in the world, she felt she was quite clearly not. What do you mean, woman? You have been voted the most beautiful woman in the entire world! You have been judged the beauty of beauties, the numero uno of pretties. As I read her self-evaluation, I can see that she doesn't think she's ugly. After all, being voted *the most beautiful woman in the world* will do that for you. But yet she has an air of dissatisfaction. To say that she is clearly not the most beautiful woman in the world reveals that she thinks other women out there are definitely more beautiful than she is. This is healthy, of course. But it also reveals that even the most beautiful woman in the world will have her hang-ups and that no one – not even the world's most beautiful woman – would dare be comfortable in her own beauty and say it out loud.

> Even the most beautiful woman in the world will have her hang-ups.

It's a truth universally acknowledged that no matter how 'beautiful' a woman may appear to the outside world, she won't like something about her body. Many women will wish that they were slimmer, while some will curse the fact that they are too skinny to fill out that dress in the right places. Some will hate their hair being bone straight and lacking in volume, while others will tame their manes into submission with straighteners that cost a fortune. The pear-shaped long for larger chests while the waifs wish they were hourglasses.

If only there was a World Wide Swap Shop of Women's Body Parts. Imagine being able to trade the bits you don't like, the bits that cause you angst, the bits that make you feel disgusted and dissatisfied. Imagine being able to exchange them for the bits of other women that you envy but that they would happily swap with you.

To a certain extent we can already do this. If we don't like our bodies, and have enough money, we can get a little help to create the perfect version of ourselves. In 2011, for example, the United States saw 13.8 million cosmetic procedures performed – up 5 per cent from the previous year.[5] From breast augmentation to nose jobs to buttock implants, millions of people were going under the knife to change the way they look. Facelifts were in the top five of cosmetic surgery procedures for the first time in that year. If you don't like your face, you can, literally, change it. Although recent years have seen an increase in the number of men altering their appearance this way, women still make up 91 per cent of those having cosmetic surgery.

Too many of us are dissatisfied with our bodies and, because we so desperately crave beauty, we will go to extreme lengths to change them. We often see ourselves as inadequate when compared to other women and beat ourselves up about it, blaming ourselves for not living up to the standard of beauty the world expects. We don't feel good enough and fall into a trap of thinking that if only we could change certain things about our appearance,

> Deep down we long to be seen as beautiful.

then we would feel happier and closer to 'beautiful'. Because that's what every woman wants. Deep down we long to be seen as beautiful. We are plagued by a sense that we will never be handed that accolade. Yet something in us so desperately wants it to be so. We beat ourselves up, always feeling like we're falling short of the essence of beauty. And this causes many of us so much pain.

I wanted to see if this was true among the Christian female friends I know; whether there is something unique to women that makes us feel inadequate. So I came up with a survey for my friends to complete. Amazingly, word spread and more than 150 women ended up taking part, telling me anonymously how they felt about their bodies. When I started to write this book, I had made some assumptions about how women see themselves. But when I probed further with the help of my mini survey, in which I started asking questions about beauty and self-image, I realized that the picture was far more devastating than I had first thought. Something is really very wrong.

Around 65 per cent of the women said they had at some point been so devastated with their own bodies that it had driven them to tears. They had cried actual tears because they were so unhappy with the bodies that we are told in the Bible are fearfully and wonderfully made. This is not OK. A further 80 per cent of the women surveyed said that they would change something about their bodies if they could. One woman said:

> We'd all change things about ourselves. Every night I dream I will wake up a size 8, with long legs, rather than a size much larger than an 8, an abnormally long upper body and short legs that look stupid on a tall girl. I want to change things about my body because I think that if I look a certain way, the rest of my life will fall into place. I'll get the right boyfriend, the right job, the right house, because things always appear easier for beautiful people. As a friend of lots of beautiful people, I know this isn't actually true, but I kid myself anyway.

Said another: 'I'd like to get back to a size 10, my boobs to be less saggy, get rid of my double chin, my boobs be smaller, the top of my thighs be thinner, the tops of my arms more toned and get rid of the fatty bits near my armpits. Need I go on?'

I read down the list of things that women would change about their bodies and imagine I am God listening to the heart cries of these women who feel imperfect. *My stomach, my knees, my nose, my fat legs.* If they were the Creator they would do a better job, they feel. They would start from scratch and get rid of their 'big nose' and 'small mouth', and trade select body parts in for 'smaller boobs', 'smaller feet' and 'less hairy arms'. I wonder how God feels about us disparaging his creation.

God made us all differently; we weren't designed to fit into one rigid mould but were designed with diversity in mind. In 1997, fashion photographer Rick Guidotti got tired of photographing models who all looked the same – who conformed to

> We weren't designed to fit into one rigid mould but were designed with diversity in mind.

a man-made stereotype of beauty – and started to see the beauty in those individuals living with genetic difference. So he began a movement called Positive Exposure, which seeks to find beauty despite the stigmas associated with genetic disorders. Right now, I am looking at his beautiful photograph of Lauren, who has albinism. It's a stunning image: her long, white hair cascading over her shoulders, her light eyelashes, her hooded eyes pointing downwards, her mouth open. She is beautiful. But the fashion industry and society will tell you that she is not. That people like Lauren could never be beautiful. That physical deformity, that genetic difference, is ugly – a departure from what is normal and acceptable. That it has no place in a beautiful world. That it should not be seen. Even Lauren's own sister – who is also a person with albinism – dyes her hair and eyelashes because she wants to conform to society's standards of acceptable beauty.

Writing in the *Huffington Post*, Rick Guidotti said:

*You have one of two reactions when you see someone who's different on the
street. You either stare, or you look away. But what if we provided an opportunity to steady your gaze long enough to see beauty in those gorgeous eyes, not
disease. Once you're able to look with a different eye, the beauty washes over
you, everything shifts, and you start to see beauty everywhere.*[6]

I love the message behind Positive Exposure. I love that it is a great
symbol of what the Kingdom of God is like – the radical idea that the
last shall be first, that *all* of us are made in God's image, no matter
what we look like. Sometimes we can be so busy trying to conform,
our eyes fixed on the narrow gate that marks out the beautiful from
the un-beautiful, that we can miss beauty. It can pass us by because we
are not looking for it in the right places, not seeing that it is all around
us, even in the unexpected places.

I think God sees beauty everywhere in his creation. And I think
God wants us to see beauty in all things too. And that does include
those things that the world *does* call beautiful. I still think that blonde
hair and blue eyes and hourglass figures are beautiful. But I also think
that we need to realize that those attributes that are none of the above
are also beautiful. Because all these things are created by Beauty. In the
Genesis account we see that God created everything and he called it all
'good'. He was pleased with what he saw. It was beautiful.

I was struck by what a friend revealed to me about a time when he
experienced something of what God must be feeling when he hears
women's unhappy thoughts about their bodies. Carl Beech, who
leads Christian Vision for Men, was praying for people in India a few
years ago when a woman came up to him who he describes as being
'incredibly beautiful'. 'In fact, she was stunning and had a compelling
sense of peace about her,' he says. He asked the interpreter what this
woman wanted prayer for and was confused when he stared back at
him, blankly. Carl asked him again what she needed prayer for. 'But
can't you see?' the interpreter asked. 'When I looked at her again,'

Carl remembered, 'I noticed for the first time that she was completely disfigured on one side of her face and that one of her arms was like a small twig where she had obviously had something like polio. I remember feeling like my head was spinning in confusion because I hadn't noticed it before. As I stood there, I felt God quietly whisper to me: "You just saw her the way I see her all the time, beautiful to me." Wow! It was, for me, a life-changing moment.'

I love this story, as it speaks to me about a God who does not look at us the way the world does. At the same time it reminds me that the way the world looks at me or judges me is not how God does. It's therefore not the thing I should struggle for, or the thing I should be most concerned with. Because it's enough to know that God rejoices over me 'with gladness' (Zeph. 3:17, NKJV). He rejoices over me because I am righteous. He doesn't sing over me because I am the right dress size. He rejoices over me because I fear him. He doesn't sing over me because I fear the numbers on the scales. He rejoices over me because I am devoted to him. He doesn't sing over me because I stick rigidly to a diet. When I really understand that God rejoices over me not because of anything I do, but because I've been made right by his grace, then I am free; no longer a slave to beauty.

> Many of us live in this constant state of dissatisfaction.

But the point is we – me included – don't understand this truth enough. Or we forget when our knowledge of God and our relationship with him are in competition with what we think are our present, daily realities. So the beauty struggle continues. Because the truth is that as women, many of us live in this constant state of dissatisfaction when we take a man's-eye instead of a God's-eye perspective on ourselves. And it all starts when we are little girls. It may not come in a moment of self-realization when drawing a portrait in school, but at some point each one of us women become aware of our bodies. The world in which we live is a broken one. As we have seen, it's a world that distorts and twists the definition of beauty and subsequently our views of ourselves. And the reality is that this picture is becoming more and more distorted and affecting women at younger ages. We'll see later the devastating effects of today's society on children. How did the world become a place in which little girls can't bear to live because they don't feel they look right? How did the world become a place where little girls are so bombarded with messages that they are not as beautiful as fashion models that they just can't take another moment of being alive? How did we arrive at a world where a 10-year-old will hang herself with her scarf because her classmates taunt her with 'fat insults'? How did the world become a place where the pressure to be beautiful robs little girls of any sense of hope?

Maybe this constant struggle with beauty exists because so often when we explore beauty, we fail to go back to its source. Our bodies, our beautiful bodies, have been made in the image and likeness of a God who is the orchestrator of beauty. So we need to find out what his beauty actually is.

The Essence of Beauty

There are times when I'm overcome by the beauty that exists in the world that God has created for us to live in, and the amazing beauty that has been crafted by the works of our hands throughout the centuries. Sometimes I'm so struck by an overwhelming sense of that which is beautiful that it takes my breath away. I feel it when I'm in a plane soaring above the cotton wool clouds that seem to glide nonchalantly through the skies like sunseekers gliding on a swimming pool. I definitely felt it standing on top of Table Mountain in Cape Town; tears welling up in my eyes as I took in the misty scenes the likes of which I had never seen. I got a sense of it sitting in a cable car looking out over the landscape of Hakone in Japan, and glimpsing the majestic Mount Fuji in the distance. When I experience beautiful scenes, something in me stirs. My mind is awakened to some transcendent truth. I feel a deep but fleeting sense of both recognition and wonder. These scenes are familiar yet strange. They speak to something deep within me, but point to something far greater than me. In essence, I recognize something of the ineffable that is beauty when I see and experience them.

I've read that 60 per cent of US 'millennials', those born between 1980 and 2000, go travelling with friends around 20 per cent more than older generations.[7] Worldwide, we are a generation constantly seeking beauty in foreign climes. We find beautiful desti-

> Worldwide, we are a generation constantly seeking beauty in foreign climes.

nations online, we book a ticket and we take our friends with us, because, more than anything, we want to experience beauty with other people, to validate the indescribable nature of what we're seeing. The jet-setting and the thrill-seeking are part of our quest to experience beauty and ultimately to experience the divine. Once we've experienced it, we want to feel it again and again and again. It's as if we are trying to make sure it's real and are attempting to understand it, to bottle it up and take a whiff of it whenever the world is ugly. Beauty has that strange paradox of being elusive yet familiar. I believe that the breathtaking beauty of the universe points to something real and something true. It is an imprint of the Creator God. He puts his stamp on things and, because he is Beauty itself, these things cannot help but be beautiful. We think that it is subjective but beauty cannot just be about the way in which I judge something. It's got to take its lead from, and find its definition in, something else entirely. I think that has got to be God. American pastor John Piper explains it well here:

Unless beauty is rooted in God's mind rather than your mind, every time you say, 'That is beautiful,' all you really mean is, 'I like that'. Unless there is a God, your praise of beauty can be no more than expressions of your own personal preferences. But I think there is in every one of you a dissatisfaction with the notion that your judgments about beauty have no more validity than your preference for coffee over tea. And I think your dissatisfaction with pure subjectivism and relativism is a remnant of God's image in your soul and evidence of his reality. It is an echo, however faint, of a voice that once called you into being.[8]

When I think of beauty, I think of my own friends – gorgeous women who are so stunning that they sometimes make me think 'wow!' Yet these women look totally different from each other. If you were to line them up, they would make a mish-mash of different shapes and sizes. But I think they're beautiful. I love Ruth's sea-blue eyes, Chi's toned physique, Kate's 'English rose' face and Abisade's elegance. I can see beauty in each of them, but these women couldn't look less alike. It's clear that beauty itself can't easily be pinned down. It is an elusive sense of a certain something that we recognize only when we see it. And this something may change depending on where and when the beholder is viewing it. It sounds like beauty therefore is something that can't be described easily.

Wordsmiths liken beauty to being artistic, attractive, beaming, bright, dazzling, elegant, enchanting, graceful, grand, picturesque, refined, resplendent, sparkling. Throughout the centuries, scientists, philosophers, photographers and fashion agencies have tried to come up with a definition of beauty that exists outside of God. Does beauty lie in a certain waist to hip ratio? Is a beautiful face beautiful because it meets some standard of symmetry? The Greek philosopher Plato also thought a lot about the nature of beauty. His Theory of Forms suggested that there are two levels of reality in existence: the reality that is seen in the physical world and a reality that exists in the abstract, in the world of Forms – which stands outside the physical. So, he said, when we see a beautiful thing in the world – a painting, a flower, a face – we identify it as beautiful because we have some understanding of the invisible, unchanging, eternal Form of Beauty. And the things we see on earth are beautiful only in so far as they participate in this abstract Form of Beauty.

I believe that we sense beauty in our 'knowers'. We know it when we see it. We can't describe it. All scientific formulae that we come up with to explain beauty will at some point be found wanting. But I 'know' I see beauty when I look at my beautiful baby goddaughter Skye. I 'know' I sense beauty in a four-part harmony. I 'know' I am looking at beauty when I stand face-to-face with the *Mona Lisa* at the Louvre in Paris. And this beauty, which I sense in my knower, this abstract, eternal, unchanging Form of Beauty, has got to come from somewhere. And I believe that somewhere is God. So what does that mean? Well, it means beauty can't be something that is dictated by the glossy magazines, nor can it be something that is prescribed by a certain society or a beholder. Beauty is an attribute of the divine and when we see it in our world, we see a stamp of God's handiwork.

Some say that beauty is a myth, that it is purely a social construct, created to make people feel bad about themselves. I believe that there *are* socially constructed, distorted views of beauty that do this. But I don't believe that true, authentic beauty is a myth. I think beauty is the essence of God. Beauty *is* God. So if beauty is God, then key to understanding whether or not I am beautiful is realizing that true beauty lies in him. The definition of beauty means nothing without him.

God's beauty is also found in diversity, in the many different types of beauty that exist in his creation. I'm reminded of 1 Corinthians 15, which is an answer to a question about what kind of body we will have when we are resurrected with Christ. Paul writes:

> *But God gives it a body as he has determined, and to each kind of seed he gives its own body. Not all flesh is the same: people have one kind of flesh, animals have another, birds another and fish another. There are also heavenly bodies and there are earthly bodies; but the splendour of the heavenly bodies is one kind, and the splendour of the earthly bodies is another. The sun has one kind of splendour, the moon another and the stars another; and star differs from star in splendour. (1 Cor. 15:38–44)*

It's stunning to think that each star is beautiful, though each star is different – and that the same goes for you and I. Though we may look completely different, each of us bears a marker of God. And God is what beauty is.

So, if beauty is what God is, then what does this mean for me on those mornings when I wake up and look at myself in the mirror? What does it mean for me if I have read that he has made *everything* beautiful in its time? It means that what I should see staring back at me is the image of God; a beautiful creation crafted by the Creator. Not a hot mess. Not a big nose or crooked teeth. But a beautiful creation. If I understand what true beauty is then I can't feel anything but beautiful. I know; it's so much easier to write this, think it, say it, isn't it? In reality, most Christian women feel they know this. This idea that we're made in the image of God is tied up with our understanding of our salvation, of how we fit into God's story. Of course I know it. I've grown up in church. I've heard about how man looks at the outside, while God looks at the inside. I've sung 'all things bright and beautiful' and been taught that I'm part of that beautiful creation. But why does all this fly out of the window so quickly when I have a bad hair day? When I just feel awful? When I'm embarrassed about my body? It's not supposed to be like this. Surely the script for Christian women should be different. Surely women who believe they are made in the image of God are satisfied with themselves? Surely as those who have been set free in Christ we no longer conform to the patterns of what we see on our television screens and the images we are bombarded with in the glossy magazines? Surely *we* know that we are beautiful? It would seem that, though this is the ideal, the reality is something else entirely. Our minds seem to be stuck in the world's pattern, so often unable to make the shift. We can't help but see ourselves with murky mirrors; it seems impossible to see through the distortion. Maybe we need a little help.

> We can't help but see ourselves with murky mirrors.

Renewing Our Eyes

There's one Bible verse that has taken on a whole new meaning for me when I come to think about my own body and when I ask whether I am beautiful or not. It is found in Romans 12:2: 'Do not conform to the pattern of this world, but be transformed by the renewing of your mind. Then you will be able to test and approve what God's will is – his good, pleasing and perfect will.'

As we have seen, so many of our views of our own beauty are tied up with the world's prescription of what beauty is – and the verse above tells me I need to stop conforming to what the world is telling me. The world's definition of beauty is illustrated in magazines and billboards and television ads. Its all-pervading message tells us that beauty is what she – the beautiful blonde on the front cover – is; and not what I am. And she is always thin.

A study by Durham University sought to find out why it is that people generally perceive a thin body as more beautiful than a fat one. Researchers Lynda Boothroyd, Martin Tovée and Thomas Pollet found people were more positive about certain body types because of Western women's 'visual diet' and also due to associative learning. The visual diet theory says that the more images there are of thin women, the more the thin body type is associated with the norm – and anything larger than that is viewed as abnormal. Western women have also internalized the idea that this thin body is associated with health, success and happiness. So we look at our own bodies through eyes whose visual diet promotes certain bodies over others. And if our own bodies deviate from that in the slightest then we can see them as negative, flawed, somehow un-beautiful.

So the world's ideal of what beauty is keeps me forever trapped in a perpetual state of being un-pretty. Because I don't quite fit into the mould. I don't quite conform to the pattern. But what Paul is telling us in this passage is: 'Who cares what the world says?' He tells us that it's not the world's pattern that we need to fit into. In this passage is a recognition that in the past we have tried to conform to the pattern. But no longer. Our task now must be to work out our own transformation. There is a way out – a transforming journey that takes effort on our part, as well as a desire no longer to conform.

The renewing process is about training our minds to think differently.

When it comes to beauty, particularly in the Western world, but also in any society, we are trapped in the pattern of our visual diet. We can't escape the images that we see every day and their frequency normalizes and then elevates certain forms of beauty. If the images we see most often are those of skinny women or red-headed women or blue women, then we will come to see skinny women or red-headed women or blue women as the norm. If we are not skinny or red-headed or blue then we feel like outsiders. I think it's possible to renew our minds. But it's not an easy thing to do. Our minds have been fed on this visual diet since we were born. That is where the Holy Spirit comes in. Yes, the renewing process is about training our minds to think differently. If I want to feel better about my body, I could embark on a visual diet of looking only at images of my own body – that way making it totally normal and beautiful!

But true, whole, lasting transformation only comes with God's help. I think we need the Holy Spirit's help in making us feel truly, utterly beautiful. In some Bible translations, the Holy Spirit is described as a 'helper'. We definitely need his help in this. Once we have accepted our bodies with the Holy Spirit's help, we also need a hand in shutting down the green-eyed monster, in order to remain secure and satisfied in ourselves. For in Hebrews 13:5 we read that we are to be content with what we have. Why does God urge us to be content? Because he knows that being jealous about what other people have – their thick, shiny hair, tiny waist, bootylicious bum, long legs – robs us of our joy. It stops us from being grateful for the beauty that we *do* possess – both inside and out. And it means that we're forgetting that he is already captivated by us. There's no longer any need to be craving beauty, because he already sees it when he looks at us. This is a continuous process of understanding. But we can't do any of it without God's help. The task is too great, too counter-cultural. But all things are possible with him. The God who created the heavens and the earth, parted the Red Sea, made the blind see and the lame walk, is surely able to help renew my little mind. With this renewal of our minds will come whole and lasting freedom – a liberation from having to conform to the world's pattern.

Wonderfully Made

Seeing myself as beautiful on those days when I really don't feel so will take real effort. It won't come naturally. And it won't be easy. But no one said that renewing our minds – training them and disciplining them to see the world differently – would be. On those days that will certainly come when I look in the mirror and find it hard to see anything beautiful, I can train my mind to focus on the amazing truths about how my body is knitted together. I can meditate on Psalm 139:14, which reminds me that 'I am fearfully and wonderfully made'. I can think about my own body as an amazing work of God's creation. And I can remind myself of some of these mind-boggling facts . . .

Every single second, my body produces 25 million cells. That's more than the number of people living in North Korea! The badoom-boom of my heart happens inside my chest around 10,000 times a day. If the 300 billion capillaries in my lungs were stretched out from one end to the other, they would cover 1,500 miles. And my bones? My little old bones are 4 times as strong as concrete. The human body – my body, your body – is astounding in its complexity, its intricacies and capabilities. It is amazingly, fearfully and wonderfully created. It is beautiful.

> Our bodies are works of art; they are marvels of biology and physics and chemistry.

So, when I ask you to think about your own body, are the first thoughts that come to mind positive or negative? When you consider your own body, do you first think about your body shape, your weight, your physique, the exterior? Why is it that we so often fail to celebrate the amazing intricacies of our fearfully and wonderfully made bodies? Why do statistics like the ones above surprise us so much?

I think we need to ask God to constantly remind us that our bodies are works of art; they are marvels of biology and physics and chemistry. They are wondrous machines, functioning like clockwork; regenerating, enduring, adapting, ever-changing, ever-growing. Our bodies are beautiful.

Prayer

Dear Beautiful Lord, you who have made me in your own image. I thank you for the beauty that I see in your creation. I thank you for the beautiful sights that my eyes have seen. I thank you for lovingly creating me as part of this creation that you yourself have called 'good'. Thank you for the privilege I have in being able to say that I am made in your image. Lord, would you help me to see it? When I look in the mirror. When I compare myself to the images in the magazines. When I walk along the street. Would your Holy Spirit help me to sense that divine beauty, which can be found in you alone? Thank you for putting something of yourself in me. Thank you that each of us bears the mark of your handiwork. Lord, I'm ashamed of the way that I have mocked your creation. I'm appalled at the way I judge other people on the way they look. God, would you help me to see everyone through a new lens; one that sees all as created in your image. Help me to recognize true beauty. Give me a glimpse of you. May I see the divine in all your created beings. Help me to see the reflection of your beauty in myself. May I see beauty everywhere. Help me to feel beautiful.
Amen

Questions to Ponder

- What is the most beautiful thing you have ever seen? What made it beautiful?
- So beauty is what God is, and we are made in God's image. But what does this mean for us on those mornings when we wake up and can't see any sign of his beauty reflected in us in the mirror?

- How do we rid ourselves of the shackles of learnt behaviours or thoughts about what is beautiful and what is not?
- Do you have to *feel* beautiful to know that you are beautiful? What difference should the knowledge make to how you feel?
- What are the challenges we face in renewing our minds?

Beauty Challenge

We are constantly bombarded with images of unrealistic beauty. Try keeping a tally of all the images of women you see in one day and split them up into those images you perceive to be 'more beautiful' than you and those who you think are 'less beautiful'. What can you learn from this?

3.

The Beauty Within

Am I beautiful? When we ask this question, so often we think only of external beauty, our physical bodies and our level of attractiveness. But beauty is not only skin deep. It's not measured by the amount of make-up we put on. So often we fail to remember that beauty is also about something that comes from some place deep inside – a beauty reflected in our character, the way we treat other people and the way in which we reflect Christ. There's more to beauty than meets the eye.

'God has given you one face and you make yourself another.'
(William Shakespeare, Hamlet*)*

'No matter how plain a woman be, if truth and honesty are written across her face, she will be beautiful.' (Eleanor Roosevelt)

'A man's face is his autobiography. A woman's face is her work of fiction.'
(Oscar Wilde)

'Your beauty should not come from outward adornment, such as elaborate hairstyles and the wearing of gold jewellery or fine clothes. Rather, it should be that of your inner self, the unfading beauty of a gentle and quiet spirit, which is of great worth in God's sight.' (1 Pet. 3:3–4)

Bare-faced in the Middle East

I recently went on a trip to Israel with Christian Aid. After a long day of travelling from London Heathrow to Tel Aviv and then jumping in a taxi – which incidentally broke down on the dual carriageway on our way to East Jerusalem – we finally arrived at our hotel. It was late in the evening when I got into my hotel room and decided I would unpack for the week. Swimming around my head were thoughts of the adventure that we were going to have; the surreal nature of the fact that I was standing in the Holy Land. I was also bracing myself for what promised to be an extremely emotive week, walking where Jesus walked but also witnessing the suffering experienced by those affected by the ongoing conflict in the region. And then suddenly I had a thought; a thought that at that moment seemed far more upsetting than anything else I was preparing to see – more tangible than the scenes of human suffering I was sure to witness in the coming days: I forgot to pack my foundation.

Panic.

Surely I could not have been so stupid. Surely I could not have forgotten my most important item. But, sure enough, I unzipped my make-up bag – my only travel essential – and opened it up to find an empty hole where my Mac Studio Fix Fluid should have been. My mind flashed back to my dresser in my room in Greenwich, south-east London, where a few hours before I had been doing my make-up, getting ready for the journey ahead. I had forgotten to pack it. I'm not sure how I can get across to you how much of a panic I was spiralled into upon realizing this catastrophe. Some pretty crazy thoughts rushed through my head. I wondered how much it would cost for me to fly back home first thing in the morning, pick up my foundation and fly back to meet the party I was travelling with in the evening. I quickly started up my laptop, connected to the Wi-Fi and Googled whether there was a Mac store in Jerusalem – or anywhere in Israel. I started plotting how on earth I could leave the group I was with, learn the Arabic or Hebrew for 'Taxi driver, get me to the Mac store!' and rush down there to find a life-saving bottle. I investigated whether it would be possible to order my foundation online and have it delivered to my hotel within 48 hours. I was willing to pay the extortionate price to make that possible.

For someone who daren't leave the house without her face on, this oversight was a tragedy of epic proportions. How could I show my bare face? Maybe I could get away with not washing off the make-up I was already wearing and seeing if it would stay on for a week?

Foundation has been my best friend for many, many years. For me, it's a tool – a weapon, if you will – to cover up my flawed skin, a way to mask the insecurities and the flaws. I was on the verge of tears, desperately disappointed that this could ruin the trip of a lifetime. At the same time looking down on my panic and realizing my dependency on this small bottle of – in effect – paint made me desperately sad.

And then a still voice came to me: 'What's the big deal? You are beautiful.'

Release. Relief.

So what if I went bare-faced for a week in Palestine? I started to think of the prospect as potentially liberating. I would push myself; I would have to be comfortable in my own skin. So, during that trip, there was no mad rush to the Mac store, no emergency flight home, no SOS. I walked around Jerusalem, prayed against the Wailing Wall, had lunch with a Bedouin family in the middle of the Judean desert, visited a mobile clinic in Beit Fajjar just outside Bethlehem – and I did it all foundation-free. I was clearly the only person who noticed I didn't have my foundation on. There were no screams of horror upon seeing my foundation-less face when I met the rest of the group for breakfast in the morning. Nobody batted an eyelid.

Clinging to Cosmetics

A little while after my Middle Eastern adventure, I went to work without any make-up on. And, do you know what? Nobody died. Nobody screamed. Again, nobody batted an eyelid. I suppressed the urge to apologize for my face – my bare, naked face – as if I had assumed people would be as offended by it as I seemed to be myself.

I had set myself the challenge of going to work one day make-up free, which, let me remind you, includes walking out of my flat, getting on a train and a bus and therefore baring my face to many, many people along the way. To give you some insight into how big a deal this was for me, we will need to delve into my history, which originates in a family full of make-up-loving women. I am the eldest of three daughters. I have five aunts on my mum's side and four on my dad's side. I am surrounded by oestrogen. And sometimes I wonder whether being surrounded by women has ingrained in me a sense of the importance of being beautiful. Like many little girls, I remember gazing up at my mother's face and thinking that hers was surely the most beautiful there ever had been. I remember wanting to grow up to be just like her. From time to time our family has a tradition of bringing out the photo albums and flicking through our collective history, which includes stunning pictures of my mum, her sisters and friends growing up – all halter necks and mini-skirts. Growing up an awkward teenager, I used to wish that I looked like her when she was my age. Something had got lost somewhere in the gene pool. Beautiful as she was, I have memories of her buying exercise videos – including those very 1980s Jane Fonda workouts – and getting up at the crack of dawn to do them. I remember evening slimming classes. I watched my aunts shopping and shopping and shopping whenever they visited us from Nigeria – a never-ending stream of clothes and shoes and cosmetics.

I had wanted to wear make-up from when I was a little girl. When each of us turned 16, the rite of passage in our house was for mum to take us to a department store where we would have a makeover and get our starter kit of make-up. I suppose that's where it all began for me. I can probably count on two hands the numbers of days I have gone make-up free since then. My rite of passage trip was my first entry into the secret club of women's beauty. The club in which you are handed the weapon of make-up; this magical gift that helps transform you from Plain Jane to Lady Fabulous.

It seems that I'm not the only one who clings on to cosmetics. A recent edition of *Stylist* magazine included a feature on the psychology of make-up, the snap judgments we make based on what people look like and the vast number of us who feel that it's only with make-up on that we can be confident in the workplace. Apparently women spend 10 working days a year getting ready for work, while 70 per cent of us feel ill-equipped without our faces on. *Stylist* cited a study called *First Impressions and Hair Impressions*, which found that 'a tide-mark of foundation indicates lack of attention to detail, heavily pencilled brows suggest cockiness and no mascara points to a potential emotional wreck'. We are judged on how pristinely we apply our make-up.

With make-up you are given permission to create a face of your choosing; or at least significantly improve the face you've got. You can make your skin flawless, make your eyes pop, give yourself that forever-flushed rouged

> With make-up you are given permission to create a face of your choosing.

look that, for some reason, we associate with health. Make-up for me is also a mask. It's quite literally a cover-up that enables me to hide my flaws from everyone. When I'm wearing this mask, I am beautiful. As far as I'm concerned, the beautiful outer adornment means that people have little inkling that there is an ugly me lurking beneath. So you can understand why I nearly chickened out of the challenge I had set myself to go to work without make-up on. That morning I showered, nervous of the bare-faced day ahead. And, after dressing, I was suddenly presented with a few minutes of free time – minutes I would normally have spent preening, smoothing, puckering, blushing, applying my face. But these minutes were spent instead staring at myself and questioning whether I was really ready to let the world see this. I felt I didn't look like myself. I felt I looked like a tired, characterless, empty, vacant version of me. I felt every blemish, every blotch on my face was visible. I felt that with this face – my real face – there was nowhere to hide. I felt vulnerable. But I'm not one to back out of a challenge. So I did it. I took my vacant, vulnerable, featureless face to work. And, like I said, nobody died. Nobody screamed. Once again, nobody batted an eyelid.

In fact, I didn't feel as ugly as I had been bracing myself for. My face felt a freedom it had rarely experienced. Loosed from the chains of foundation, lip gloss, blusher, eyeliner and mascara, it could breathe. It was not being smothered. It was *seen*. I was *seen*. Just as I was. No pretence. No elaboration. No hiding. Just. Me.

A few weeks later, I saw that Adios Barbie, a body image campaigning website, were asking people to send in photos of their make-up free faces for an online gallery for their 'bare-faced and beautiful' campaign in honour of National Eating Disorders Awareness Week. I wanted to test myself and see if I had truly overcome being a slave to make-up. Could I really bare for the whole world, not just my colleagues, to see my face? Before I could change my mind, I sent in my photo – which was picked to appear on the online gallery. I took a deep breath before sharing it on my Facebook page and encouraging others to join me in going make-up free. I was taken aback by the comments and wondered if they were being genuine or not. To me, my natural face still did not look great. But it seemed people really liked the real me.

On the Face of It

My experiment with my make-up free face reminded me of a story that has haunted me for some years – a story about a woman whose face was literally stripped away.

I first came across Katie Piper's story on a Channel 4 documentary. Katie was beautiful; the kind of blonde beautiful that doesn't threaten, but possesses those sparkly blue eyes that invite you in. The kind of beautiful that makes you smile. All the way through school, she was the one all the boys had a crush on. When she left school she decided to take everyone's advice and become a model. Building up her portfolio, she also did a bit of TV presenting on the side. The camera loved her. Because she was beautiful. One day she met Danny on a social networking site. They had a whirlwind romance and within a couple of weeks he had told her he loved her. He lavished her with gifts, spoiled her. But it was almost suffocating. And then one day he flipped, unleashing the animal that had been lurking beneath. Raping her and attacking her in a hotel room, he threatened to kill members of her family if she ever let anyone know. Terrified, violated, humiliated and broken, she thought she had sunk to her lowest point. That was, until he stole her beautiful face. One day, walking along the road near her flat, Katie was approached by a young man – a friend of Danny's –

I'll never forget her face, eaten away by acid.

who threw acid in her face as he got close to her. Her beautiful face. The face that she had built her career on, the face that the boys in school had loved, was now being eaten through by the acid in the most excruciating manner.

I cannot for one minute imagine how devastating it must have been for her to go from beauty to burns victim within just a few earth-shattering moments. I cannot imagine what it must have been like for her to know that someone planned the attack in order to rob her of her identity, to steal her joy, to ruin her life. I can't imagine what it must have been like for her to go from having faced the constant attention of men, to having her scars scrutinized and stared at every time someone glanced in her direction. I'll never forget her face, eaten away by acid, her fight for survival and her bravery as she also experienced the terrifying reality of coming face to face with the people who had done this to her in the courtroom.

She writes in her book *Beautiful* that she often felt like a 'freak'. What must that have been like? Thinking back on her time in hospital, she wrote: 'For some reason, I kept telling everyone about my old life, too. I was desperate for them to know I hadn't always been this way. "Hello! My name's Katie, and I'm a model," I said over and over to the nurses. "I know you can't tell now, but I used to be pretty!"'[9] Katie's story, though tragic, is ultimately a story of redemption. Though she loses what the world would have classed as her external beauty, her model looks, she gains an understanding of true beauty that few of us will ever be able to comprehend. And through that painful journey from model to burns victim to true beauty she draws close to God, the one in whom true beauty is found. She writes: 'I'd woken up. I'd seen what was truly important in life, and found a strength I never knew I had. All the pain and suffering, the horror and the terror, the tears and screams – I'd survived it all. Yes, I was a new Katie, but that was a good thing. Through it all, I'd learnt that kindness and love are the most wonderful things of all, and from that moment on I knew my life was going to be beautiful, in every single way.'

Katie's story is a nightmare that I would never want to live through. Our faces can often be our pride and joy. They bear a mark of our unique identity. A beautiful woman is described as such primarily because she has a gorgeous face. In *Doctor Faustus*, Christopher Marlowe describes the face of the mythological Helen of Troy as that which 'launched a thousand ships'. Our faces are one-of-a-kind. They contain our eyes, the windows to our souls and the peepholes to the outside world.

I like that I can enhance the face that God has given me every morning with a bit of make-up. Perhaps it's the bit I feel I have the most control over. Perhaps I like it because when I look at my face, I see that I'm my mother's daughter – and I am increasingly seeing a resemblance. When I look at my face, I'm not just looking at my face, but looking at my past, my present and hopefully my future. My face communicates what I'm feeling. It lets the world know when I'm angry; when I'm flirting; when I'm upset, afraid, overjoyed.

> I fake it, presenting my masked face as an offering to the god of aesthetics.

As I've said, during the course of writing this book, I've realized that I wear make-up like a mask, in which I hide my face for fear of what people might think of it. I have been trapped in a dependence on this mask as the only way in which I can be judged beautiful; because I feel that underneath is something unacceptable, sub-standard. I have dark bags under my eyes, my skin is flawed and my cheeks of course do not naturally flush. So I paint it all on. I fake it, presenting my masked face as an offering to the god of aesthetics. It took the mask being literally stripped away from her for Katie to realize that inner beauty and inner goodness are what matters. How futile it seems when all is said and done to be painting an artificial mask to seek approval from others, when that's really not all that life is about. When I wear a people-pleasing mask, or I pretend I'm someone else to try to fit in with the 'right' crowd, I'm looking at the outer rather than the things that display inner beauty.

Even in church, it's not easy to allow the mask to slip. We talk of being a community of people who are open, honest and vulnerable with each other. But there is something in us that wants to keep back the ugliest truths about us. We don't want to reveal anything we think could negatively impact what people think about us. So we keep all the bad stuff locked inside, like the mess we stuff into cupboards in our homes when visitors drop by before we have properly cleaned up. We ourselves know the mess is there, and it niggles away at us as we hold our breath and pray that it won't all spill out, leaving the bad stuff out in full display of polite society.

But it can be truly liberating to let the junk out and let people know that we feel ugly sometimes, that we're ashamed of our bodies or are suffering from crippling anxiety and comparison. Writing this book for me has been like simultaneously allowing the mask to slip and ripping off a plaster. As a newspaper journalist at heart, I am comfortable with telling other people's stories, exploring their lives and successes and failures and re-telling them in newsprint. Here I am, however, telling you what lies beneath the mask I present to the world; no longer the objective observer, but the flawed protagonist. Though it is at times painful, and I occasionally have to psyche myself up to big reveals, I'm revelling in this newfound honesty and open-ness. At times I am enjoying telling you about the things I like least about myself. Because this book isn't one long therapy session just for me. It's a tool through which I hope that you too might be liberated to talk about the things hidden in the dark places that cause you the most anxiety, and to come clean when you face feelings of inadequacy, shame and low self-esteem.

Recognizing Inner Beauty

I'm trying to dig a little deeper into why I have clung to cosmetics and why I'm so afraid of being 'un-beautiful'. I think what lies at the heart is a fear that maybe there is nothing beautiful underneath. I strive to achieve the mask of beauty because I'm not sure that inner beauty exists; or I'm not convinced that it is more important than outer beauty. When people say 'she's beautiful on the inside', I always assume that they mean 'ugly on the outside'; that inner beauty is dowdy and plain and something we say about people who are nice enough, but just do not fit the 'pretty pattern'. Just like outer beauty, this inner beauty seems hard to define anyway. When I asked people to say what they thought was meant by the phrase 'inner beauty', they came up with a whole range of different answers – which, on the surface, seemed to have no similarities between them: 'Someone who gives everything and expects nothing, always putting others' needs before their own,' said one friend. 'Someone who seems to smile from the inside out', 'someone who exudes wonder and a spirit of thankfulness and compassion', said others. 'A person who shows love and goodness towards all humankind and radiates outwards', 'someone with a heart you would love to have'.

> Real, authentic beauty is about issues of the heart, those things that you can't see when you look in the mirror.

The words they were describing were qualities that were 'good', and reflected the most beautiful characteristics of human nature. Real, authentic beauty is about issues of the heart, those things that you can't see when you look in the mirror. So talking about 'inner beauty' goes way beyond finding something nice to say about 'outer ugliness'. Inner beauty is about that which is divine, a character that reflects the beauty of God and a nature that radiates it.

'Your beauty should not come from outward adornment, such as elaborate hairstyles and the wearing of gold jewellery or fine clothes,' 1 Peter 3:3 reminds us. Our beauty has got to come from some other place. Yet, in my craving to be beautiful, I have concentrated on the outer – the make-up and the clothes and the hair – rather than cultivating what's beautiful on the inside. I've been amazed to find how little difference the outer makes to how people see me anyway. People who think I'm a beautiful person see me as a beautiful person regardless of what I've done to my face or my body that day.

But does that mean that I should never give myself a little extra help? That I shouldn't enhance what God has given me, to make it shine? Am I to let my body fall into disrepair because all that matters is on the inside. Well, Paul writes in 1 Corinthians 3:16 that our bodies are temples. What does that mean?

In my visit to Israel, I spent time at the Wailing Wall – the western wall of the Jewish Temple talked about in the Old Testament, standing majestic in the Old City of Jerusalem. It is one of the world's holiest sites and as I stood, my head covered, with my hands pressed against the warm white stone in prayer, I thought about what had gone on there centuries before. This temple belonged to God, but, because it was so sacred, a vast amount of time and money was spent in adorning it to make it presentable to the Lord. In 1 Chronicles 29:2 King David says: 'With all my resources I have provided for the temple of my God – gold for the gold work, silver for the silver, bronze for the bronze, iron for the iron and wood for the wood, as well as onyx for the settings, turquoise, stones of various colours, and all kinds of fine stone and marble – all of these in large quantities.' That's a lot of outer adornment, and it's all done so that the temple is beautiful and fitting for God.

Amber Dobecka from Texas believes that we should look after our bodies in the same way as the Jews looked after the temple. Years as an athlete and a cheerleader taught her the importance of nutrition. Now a qualified fitness instructor, she believes our bodies can be the vessel through which God's beauty shines. 'To me, exercising and shaping my body to be the best "me" I can be is a way I can glorify God for his creation,' she tells me. It's like an act of worship. God wants us to live abundant lives, and we can't do that without our health. Working out on a regular basis takes discipline, which tells God that we care about the body he gave us, and we want to cherish it.

Many of us don't know enough about taking care of our bodies or we don't have time to do it. One of the most common things I hear from women is they're too busy to work out or eat healthy. Many times, they're taking care of their husband or kids, with little time to focus on themselves. It's important for women to be educated on how to implement a healthy lifestyle not only for themselves, but also for the rest of their family.

I get that we need to look after our bodies. But on those cold, early mornings when I am motivated enough to drag myself out of bed and head to the gym for a spin class – in my opinion the most tortuous exercise devised by humans – I'm really doing it for myself. Because I want to be slim. Because I want to be pretty. Because I want to be beautiful. God doesn't often come into my exercise plan.

Amber tells me it's OK for me to want to be beautiful. 'That's how God made us,' she says. 'We're supposed to want to look pretty and be noticed – and that's OK.' She's not happy with women in church who judge others because they wear make-up or spend time on their hair. 'They feel it's sinful to place any value on external beauty,' she says. 'What they're missing is that God created women to reflect his beauty "in his image". But we can't become obsessed with appearance at the expense of our heart.'

> God doesn't often come into my exercise plan.

And this is what Paul is getting at in 1 Peter. It's OK to look after your body, to adorn it and make it look nice, but that is not where our beauty lies. 'Rather,' he writes, 'it should be that of your inner self, the unfading beauty of a gentle and quiet spirit.' That's what's of great worth in God's sight. How often have you seen or met someone who is 'beautiful' by the world's standards, but who becomes ugly when you start to realize that their heart is dark, unkind and cruel? 'When you're pretty on the inside, you'll glow,' Amber tells me. 'You can't glow if you have an ugly heart.' It's what's on the inside that counts. It's the beauty within that God cares about, not the outward prettiness as dictated by whatever temporal socially constructed definition you are judging it against. And that gentle, quiet spirit? That comes from being totally secure and at ease in who you are and who God's made you to be. It is that graceful assurance that you are OK, that you're beautiful and totally in tune with God; with no need for a frantic search for adornment that will prove you are. That is inner beauty. And there is of course no greater example of inner beauty in human form than Jesus Christ.

Was Jesus Beautiful?

Picture Jesus. I'm guessing that, when you think about what he looked like, you think of the guy in *Jesus Christ Superstar* or *The Greatest Story Ever Told*. You're probably thinking of an attractive man with luscious long locks, a beard trimmed to perfection and piercing blue eyes. Oh and he's definitely white. This guy is probably what the majority of us conjure up in our minds if we're ever asked to picture our Saviour. Because that's what an archetype of a hero might look like in our cultural context. The Jewish people would have been expecting their equivalent of a hero who looked the part when they thought about the Messiah that was to come. But, in so many ways, the Jesus that came was not like the person that they had expected. Because Jesus was not beautiful. Not as the world expected him to be anyway. If you think about it, Jesus probably would not have been cast in a movie to play himself. He would not have been deemed pretty enough. Jesus was not George Clooney. He wasn't Eric Bana or Brad Pitt or Robert Pattinson or any other of these beautiful male works of God's creation. I know this because the Bible tells us so:

> *He had no beauty or majesty to attract us to him,*
> *nothing in his appearance that we should desire him.*

He was despised and rejected by mankind,
  a man of suffering, and familiar with pain.
Like one from whom people hide their faces
  he was despised, and we held him in low esteem.
Surely he took up our pain
  and bore our suffering,
yet we considered him punished by God,
  stricken by him, and afflicted. (Is. 53:2–4)

I wonder whether I would give Jesus a second look if I saw him walking down the street. I wonder whether he would be the type of person that would be invisible to me; or the type of person that I would avoid sitting next to on a bus. The verses above tell us that at least during his crucifixion, people 'hid their faces' from him. Instead of being drawn towards him, he repelled people. Despised, rejected. We find it uncomfortable to believe that this passage is actually talking about Jesus' physical beauty – or lack thereof. And that's precisely because of the way we have been conditioned to believe that external beauty is equal to goodness. And since Jesus was perfect, our minds tell us that he must have also *looked* perfect too. That's what artists throughout the centuries have depicted him as – beautiful. There is a beauty bias that exists in human societies in which people deemed more attractive do better in just about every area of life. In what has been described as the 'beauty-as-good' theory,[10] we associate attractiveness with positive attributes. Attractive people earn more, they are assumed to be more friendly, they are less likely to be found guilty in court and are given more lenient sentences when they are.

> I wonder whether I would give Jesus a second look if I saw him walking down the street.

Psychiatrist Dr Igor Elman has even suggested that prettier babies are more loved by their mothers.[11]

As humans, we associate beauty with goodness. And since Jesus was the ultimate example of 'good', our minds find it hard to believe that his appearance was not so good. But that in itself is beautiful. Because this man was our beautiful Saviour God.

Jesus' beauty is beyond pretty.

As fifteenth-century century Nicholas of Cusa wrote: 'O! Lord; and all beauty that can be conceived is less than the beauty of Your Face. All faces have beauty; but they are not beauty itself. But Your Face, O! Lord, has beauty, and this having is being. Hence, Your Face is Absolute Beauty.'[12]

When we sing of Jesus' beauty, we're not talking about how great he looked. Song lyrics speak of a beauty that can be found only in the majesty of the divine – the beauty that creates; the beauty that is light and power and sacrifice. Jesus' beauty is beyond pretty. He, Beauty, is the one who gave his life that we might be totally free. And this freedom includes a freedom from un-pretty thoughts – about ourselves, about our bodies and about other people. This God in his un-prettiness on this earth showed that it's really not about the outward appearance. It didn't matter what he looked like. He was divine, inner beauty embodied. In 2 Corinthians 4:6, we read that God, 'made his light shine in our hearts to give us the light of the knowledge of God's glory displayed in the face of Christ'. Isaiah tells us that there was nothing special about him physically, but the paradox is that Jesus' face displayed God's glory in all its brilliance. Though mankind rejected him and turned their faces away from him, he was, and is, Beauty itself. The outward adornment was just a covering for something beautiful inside – something that had nothing to do with the physical.

When we talk about beauty as people of faith, we are really speaking about some 'other' beauty; beauty totally uncorrupted. Beauty itself. It's as if we are trying to peer through the outer layers into what it is that we are actually calling beautiful. Beauty, when it comes to God, means far more than beauty. That's why Jesus could be unattractive in humankind's eyes but yet at the same time be the most beautiful person that ever walked the face of this earth.

Was Jesus beautiful? No. Was Jesus Beauty? Yes.

Walford writes in *The Beauty of God*:[13] 'A broken beauty can be a redemptive beauty, which acknowledges suffering while preserving hope . . . For the Christian artist the incarnation of Christ provides a basis to engage with integrity both beauty and ugliness, pleasure and pain.'

When we look in the mirror and those lies start to creep in about ugliness, we need to remember that, in that instance, we might not be beautiful. No, maybe we are not beautiful, not on the outside, not beautiful as the world might think. But do you know what we are? We are Beauty. We are Beauty because the one who created us and breathed his life into us is Beauty. So we have inside us an inner beauty. As I write these words, I hear how they must sound. It's easy for me to type them and jump up and down inside and believe that I will never again think that I am not beautiful. I also know that it will take more than just reading a few words for it to sink in. But I pray that one day it will. I pray that one day we will all be free from the feeling that we are somehow inadequate or somehow not beautiful enough; free from thinking that it is outer beauty alone that matters.

I think there is a reason why Jesus was not beautiful. He could just as well have been a first-century pin-up if God wanted to reveal himself to us in that way. No one would have blamed him for casting a dreamy Jim Caviezel-type as Mel Gibson did in *The Passion of the Christ*. God was trying to draw people to Jesus, right? He was trying to usher them into the Kingdom of God. And humans are drawn to attractive people. We cry when beautiful people die: Diana, Marilyn Monroe, James Dean. We are outraged when blonde, blue-eyed cute kids like Madeleine McCann are snatched from their parents. We feel more empathy because beautiful things shouldn't suffer. But Jesus, the beautiful and un-beautiful, was like one from whom men turned their faces away, although he was God in human form.

What if we were to see the *imago dei* – beauty – in everyone; not just the Princess Dianas or the James Deans of this world? What if we were to take off the glasses that cause us to see beauty through an arbitrary, man-made, culturally defined lens and look purposefully for the beauty of God, to search for inner beauty in others? It could change everything.

More Than Just a Beauty Queen

I've always been a little intimidated by Esther in the Bible. Because I have always read her story as one of a stunningly beautiful woman, winning the heart of a king and getting her own way. I never really related to her. But as I've grown older, I've realized that physical beauty is only part of Esther's story.

After Queen Vashti is deposed from the throne for disobeying King Xerxes, he sets out on a search to find a replacement. 'Let a search be made for beautiful young virgins for the king . . . let beauty treatments be given to them. Then let the young woman who pleases the king be queen instead of Vashti' (Esth. 2:2–4).

After the pampering, prepping and preening, Esther – an orphan from the Jewish tribe of Benjamin – is judged the most beautiful and wins the heart of the king. When a plot to execute all the Jews comes to light, Esther is placed in an uncomfortable position of having to take action. Of course she is reluctant at first – just like you or I would be. She probably doubts herself, her power and her influence. And she knows that speaking up could see her killed. But her cousin Mordecai says in Esther 4:4: 'For if you remain silent at this time, relief and deliverance for the Jews will arise from another place, but you and your father's family will perish. And who knows but that you have come to your royal position for such a time as this?'

From somewhere, Esther musters up an immense amount of bravery and says: 'If I perish, I perish'; words that always give me goose-bumps because they display a complete commitment to God's purposes even if it means her destruction. They reflect a selflessness that I often beat myself up about not possessing. Her actions eventually save the Jewish people. Her looks are not the reason we remember her. Beauty is only part of her story. She

We are here to be world-changers.

is freed from her life as an orphan for a purpose: to save the Jewish people. The same is true for us – beauty is only part of our stories. We are here to be world-changers – to affect those we come into contact with for the better.

The account of Esther's life is about much more than a beauty pageant winner being forced to think about people other than herself. It's Esther's inner beauty that is the thing we are supposed to be focusing on here; her grace, courage, strength, confidence and integrity. These qualities are beautiful and the story reveals that she is not born with them. She has to wrestle with some of the decisions she makes and is encouraged and challenged by those around her.

In the same way, our lives as followers of Christ should be a life-long process of developing and cultivating our inner beauty. For us that means becoming more Christ-like, the best example of the beauty within. 'And we all, who with unveiled faces contemplate the Lord's glory,' we read in 2 Corinthians 3:18, 'are being transformed into his image with ever-increasing glory, which comes from the Lord, who is the Spirit.' I am most beautiful when I look most like the image of Christ, when my character is beautiful because it reflects his. The passage makes clear that we *are* being transformed. It is happening because we are in relationship with God; and it is all happening with the help of the Holy Spirit. The Apostle Paul has come up with nine helpful markers of that beautiful character, known as the Fruits of the Spirit. They are: love, joy, peace, patience, kindness, goodness, faithfulness, gentleness and self-control.

Prayer

Dear Lord,
I'm sorry for the times when I have judged people, including myself, on what is outside rather than seeing the person inside. I'm amazed that you would make me in your image and that you would continue to transform me to ever-reflect your glory. Help me to see that glory and recognize the fruits of the spirit, becoming more and more like you with the help of your holy spirit.
Amen

Questions to Ponder

- How would you describe inner beauty?
- Do you think the world looks at outer beauty and inner beauty in equal measure?
- Is it harder to be beautiful on the inside or beautiful on the outside?

- What will you do practically to nurture the beauty within?
- In what way do you think you could change your 'world' for the better in the next twelve months?

4.

Beauty Control

*Am I beautiful? In our quest for beauty we go to extreme lengths to try
to control what our bodies look like. We may put ourselves through tough
beauty regimes, or control the amount of food that we eat – either by over-
eating or starving ourselves. But in attempting to control our bodies we can
find ourselves spiralling out of control, sometimes plunging into dangerous
waters.*

'If a woman has long hair, it is a glory to her.' (1 Corinthians 11:15, NKJV)

'The amount of maintenance involving hair is genuinely overwhelming.
Sometimes I think that not having to worry about your hair anymore is
the secret upside of death.' (Nora Ephron, *I Feel Bad About My Neck*)

'They loathed all food and drew near the gates of death. Then they cried to
the LORD in their trouble, and he saved them from their distress. He sent out
his word and healed them; he rescued them from the grave.' (Ps. 107:18–22)

Hair: Our Crowning Glory

I lie awake, head throbbing, brain pulsating through my forehead as my body protests against me for the trauma I put my hair through yesterday. My hair. Its strands pulled tightly away from my scalp, forced into corn rolls. Its kinks and curls suppressed into smooth, artificial plaited rows to allow Someone Else's hair to sit flatly on top of my head, making me look just like said Someone Else. It's not my hair. It did not sprout from my head in the original sense, but it belongs to me. I paid a good price for it.

I am jealous of men. Men with their carefree heads, free from the weight I carry on mine. I see their scalps, their short, shaved baby hairs barely peeping through and I wonder how it feels to have no barrier between the skin on your head and the cool, smooth cotton of a pillowcase. I wish I had the freedom to move like they do in their sleep. Tossing and turning when they get uncomfortable in one position. My neck aches from staying rigid, for fear of causing further pain to my angry head. The hair that had spent six hours in the salon being pulled and yanked away from my head cries out in pain as I try to lay my head to rest following the troubles of yesterday, forcing it back towards the scalp from which it had nearly been separated. I never thought slumber could be so painful, I think to myself as I reach for another painkiller and wash it down with the water from the glass on my bedside table. You never thought? My hair reminds me, as it brings to mind the countless times we have been through this painful routine following a day at the salon. Each time I tell myself 'never again'. Each time I forget. And when I get bored of my current style, envious of the ebony beauties sporting their latest 'dos, or when the tracks start to show through as if my natty weave has given up and said 'I'm done', I take myself off to the hairdressers again for the next pain-inducing ritual. One painful encounter I recall as I lie awake in the near-darkness is of a sixteen-hour stretch spent with my head bent between a woman's knees as she slowly created the eighteen-inch 'pick and drop' plaits I had thought seemed like a good idea at the time. This was it, I thought. The hairstyle that would bring me all my heart's desires. But, instead, all it brought me was a crick in the neck and a bum so numb it might as well not have been there. But just like childbirth, I imagine, I forgot about the pain when I stared at my long locks in the mirror, watching the plaits swish from side to side as I swayed my head. I forgot about the pain when people commented on my hair.

Black women would ask where I had done it, noting they would try it out the next time. White friends would look at me puzzled, on seeing my new 'do, and ask: 'You look different. What's different about you? Did you do something different?' And I'd say nonchalantly: 'Oh, I just had my hair done.' And pretend it was no big deal. Sixteen hours sat on the floor, with my head bent between a woman's knees. No big deal.

The early birds are starting to tweet outside and I glance at the alarm clock – 5.30 a.m. It will soon be time for work, time to start another week and face the troubles it brings with it. I close my eyes, exhale and try to force myself to forget the dull pain that keeps hammering against my temple, the small pockets of agony as my skin is stretched at points all over my head. No use.

And suddenly I sit up, angry. Raging at the injustice of it all; the fact that I cannot get a good night's sleep just because I have had my hair done the day before, tried to change my appearance, in search of the perfect look, the perfect weave, the perfect me. The search to be beautiful. I try to count the number of hours, the amount of money that I have spent so far in my lifetime on changing my hair from its natural state. Why? Because I remember the tears as a little girl when my hair was being combed through. The pulling and the yanking, the war between the comb and my Afro hair, which refused to give in. I remember the pain as my mother or a grandmother or an aunty would score across the scalp with the sharp point of a fine-tooth comb, separating it into sections to be plaited into all sorts of intricate designs that left my head red raw. Or tied into a Mickey Mouse-ear-shaped catastrophe. I would wear my Mickey Mouse hair to school, while other white little girls would be taunting me with their pigtails. Oh, how I longed for a tail that would swish and swoosh in the wind. The pigtail girls would touch my hair, look curiously at it, and then laugh, saying: 'Your hair doesn't move. It just stays where it is, it's so wiry and springy.' I dreamed of having long, flowing hair that I could run my fingers through. I daydreamed about having hair as long as Rapunzel's. But then I would awake with a jolt. Because, back in reality, my hair was neither long nor flowing. It was tough and unruly, 'kinky' and 'nappy'.

> I daydreamed about having hair as long as Rapunzel's.

I remember the amazement the day my mum first took me, aged 8, to get my hair 'relaxed' – a chemical straightening procedure. While sitting there with the cold, stinging, white cream on my head, I thought that at the end I would look like Princess Jasmine from *Aladdin*, that my hair would be long and straight and would flow in the wind. The end product was not as I had hoped. I still didn't look like Aladdin's princess. But my hair was a lot more manageable, a lot straighter and freer. It didn't quite look like the other girls' hair in my class, but I was much happier with this halfway house.

In 2009, US comedian Chris Rock made a documentary film called *Good Hair*, which delved into the $9 billion black hair industry that had previously been a secret obsession among black women. I remember watching the film for the first time, my mouth aghast; relieved that the secret was out about our ridiculous hair regimes, but also ashamed and appalled at our collective unhealthy obsession. Chris Rock decided to explore the issue after his 5-year-old daughter Lola asked him: 'Daddy, how come I don't have good hair?' That was his first glimpse into the sense of un-prettiness and dissatisfaction that forms part of the black woman's psyche when it comes to her hair and her beauty. Because our hair is different, it is seen as other – strange, foreign, ugly. And because of that we go to extraordinary lengths to change its natural state or to simply fake it.

I live not far from Deptford in south-east London, where I have been going to have my hair done since I was a child. In one afternoon in the hairdressers, you can see life in all its glory. Deptford is rich in its vibrancy. It is a melting pot of cultures – its young men strutting down the high street, its old men reminiscing on doorsteps. You will also find there: artisan creatives and yodelling market stall-holders, Vietnamese restaurant owners, Chinese shoe sellers, Asian halal butchers, Caribbean bakers and Cockney fruit and veg vendors. But the salons of Deptford are some of the most exciting places you will experience.

They are also stressful: your hairdresser will have no qualms about screaming at the colleague she is having a disagreement with right over your head. The TV will be blaring out the latest Nollywood (Nigerian Hollywood) drama, complete with highly implausible but gripping plotline. Your head will be forced under a cold tap because the plumbing isn't quite working at the moment. Your treatment will pause momentarily while your hairdresser rummages through the bags of wares – DVDs, shoes, perfume, handbags – being sold by sellers who come right into the shop to show you what they've got this week. Customers and colleagues will share their life stories – their immigration status, their children's behaviour, their cheating boyfriend, their sick mother back home. This is where life happens. In the weaves, and the chemical relaxers and the plaits and the colourings. And at the heart of this hubbub are women who are getting their hair done because they want to be beautiful. We recognize in each other the importance of that. The hairdressers know that, whatever is going on in our lives, we all crave that boost – that momentary, beautiful feeling when we look in the mirror at our new hairstyle. Beautiful.

Black women will all have memories of the pain caused by having our tough hair done when we were children – combed through, scalps scraped and scored, the sting of the chemical relaxers; and the constant hassle and the joy of the Black Woman's Hair Upkeep. Having black hair is painful, expensive, time-consuming and occasionally wonderful. It is a significant part of our lives as black women. But all women have a hair story.

> This is where life happens. In the weaves, and the chemical relaxers and the plaits and the colourings.

You could be a tree-hugger sporting dreadlocks. You may have opted for a short, sassy style to save you time and give you that power look in the boardroom. Maybe you chopped it all off when you became a full-time mum. Maybe you dyed your hair blonde because you thought it would help you find love. Maybe you turned brunette for the same reason. Maybe you wash it every day. Maybe you're a slave to the hair straighteners. Maybe you regularly visit the salon or maybe you opt for DIY. Whatever you do, you have a hair story.

In some cultures and religious traditions, the story of a woman's hair is one of attraction and sexuality. It's why women in strict Muslim traditions wear burkas or hijabs to conceal their hair – as do nuns in Catholic traditions or some other Christian traditions including the Brethren, Amish and Mennonites.

Many Christian groups who practise head covering for women today base this practice on 1 Corinthians 11:4–6 in which Paul writes: 'Every man who prays or prophesies with his head covered dishonours his head. But every woman who prays or prophesies with her head uncovered dishonours her head – it is the same as having her head shaved. For if a woman does not cover her head, she might as well have her hair cut off; but if it is a disgrace for a woman to have her hair cut off or her head shaved, then she should cover her head.'

And later on in the chapter, we read in verse 15 that 'if a woman has long hair, it is her glory? For long hair is given to her as a covering.' We need to understand the cultural and historical context of the verse rather than simply transferring it to our churches today. A woman with a shaved head was likely to be a prostitute, or a slave who had been shamed. In the culture, for a woman to have long, flowing hair, signified that she had a 'sexually loose lifestyle'.[14] Paul didn't want Christian women mistaken for such women. So he suggested that they should keep their hair long, but make sure they tie it up in order not to send out the wrong message.

Hair can do that – send out messages. In film, television and theatre, there are a number of familiar tropes, metaphors for what a woman does with her hair and what it illustrates. In *Grease*, the prim and proper Sandra D sports a cutesy, controlled bob. But when she transforms into the leather-clad Sandy, her hair is permed into tight, mischievous curls and hairsprayed into its big-haired glory. In the high school rom-com *She's All That* the supposedly unattractive Laney has a scraped-back serious hairdo in her 'before' scenes and following her transformation is rocking a fun, sparky brunette bob.

> For centuries, women's hair has been worshipped as a sign of our beauty.

Many films have scenes in which a woman slowly, tantalizingly, takes off her glasses, takes out the pin that is holding her hair up in a tight bun, letting her long locks blow in the made-for-the-scene breeze. For centuries, women's hair has been worshipped as a sign of our beauty and a way in which we make statements about our identity, our mood and who we want to be. Our hair can define who we are. But this belief that your hair can define you – that it can make you happy or sad or successful – can result in what Michelle van Loon in *Christianity Today* describes as 'hair-dolatry'. Michelle realized the extent of her own obsession with her hair when she was invited on a trip to Africa with a friend to look at the work of a non-profit organization. She wrote: 'Instead of a dewy-eyed, "I'll go wherever God sends me," or even the sturdy old-stall tactic, "Let me pray about it," my first thought was, *How will I blow dry my hair?*'

Our hair really is the crowning glory for many of us. If our hair is right, then we feel good. If we're having a bad hair day, it feels like nothing will go right. In my mini-survey, I discovered that women are generally happier with their faces and their hair than other parts of their bodies. Just 30 per cent of my respondents said they were happy with or 'loved' their body. That shot up to 60 per cent when it came to their hair. And it's also the part of our beauty that we seem to have the most control over. Viren Swami, psychologist at the University of Westminster in London, and an excitingly named 'attraction expert' for YouBeauty, said: 'Because hair is so malleable, it can give women a feeling of control over their bodies which they don't otherwise have.'[15] It's why so many of us go to the hairdressers when we feel we need a lift. We need a fix and that's one way we know we can get it.

I know I spend hours and hours on my hair, buying endless hair products, spending too much time and money at the salon. Maybe I do so because I believe my hair is my 'crowning glory', that it is the most prominent marker when it comes to judging whether or not I am beautiful. Good hair will get me far. So I need to do everything in my power to ensure it's right, to bring it into submission, to control it.

My relationship with food, however, is less easy to control.

Food Anxiety: A Familiar Story

We live in a world obsessed with food. From *Masterchef* to *Hell's Kitchen*, we are fed a constant stream of mouth-watering images of food created to perfection. But then we are told these delicious foods are on the *You Are What You Eat* banned list. We see countless images of stunningly beautiful women and then we turn the page and are let into their diet secrets. Beyoncé is on a maple-syrup diet, Cheryl Cole doesn't eat after 5 p.m., Madonna follows a macrobiotic bacteria-boosting diet and Rihanna sees carbs as the enemy.

> I talk more about food and dieting than I do about the saving, transforming good news of Jesus Christ. Why is that?

I talk more about food and dieting than I do about the saving, transforming good news of Jesus Christ. Why is that? Maybe because it's what is expected. While speaking openly and unashamedly about your faith may see you labelled a Bible basher, swearing by the latest diet fad in which you eat a lettuce leaf for breakfast, two for lunch and throw in a third for dinner makes you somewhat of a heroine. Such self-control! Although dieting and food regimes are the outworking of very deep personal issues, we as women feel comfortable talking about them with each other, at least on a superficial level. Because society expects women to talk about these things, and it encourages us to. Of the many women I spoke to, the vast majority said they had been on a diet. Dieting seems to be a part of many women's lives, whether they need to lose weight or not. Maybe we go on diets because we feel we are supposed to. It's what women do, isn't it? It is a practice of the sisterhood, and sharing the trials and tribulations of our latest diets gives us something to talk about. It's a female bonding thing – like sport is for so many men.

Food and dieting form part of an oath of understanding between women. And in church, just like outside the church, this bond actually promotes food anxiety, rather than something wholly positive. Because if we know that we're supposed to watch what we eat and that most women are on diets, we know – or think we know – that others will be watching what we eat too. But in churches around the world, food is an important part of fellowship and celebration. We feel eyes on us when we go for another cookie at the end of church. One woman reveals how isolated she feels having an unhealthy relationship with food and living in a world where there is food, food everywhere. 'You can't separate food from life,' she tells me. 'It's there on all major occasions, good and bad, social situations as well as everyday life. Food can be used as a reward and as a punishment. For someone with an eating disorder, food is terrifying, regardless of whether you are bulimic, anorexic or a compulsive eater. It consumes your world, becomes all you think about.'

Even if we don't suffer from an eating disorder, I know for one that I'm guilty of playing up my healthy eating because I sense that my contribution to the bring and share lunch will be scrutinized. What lies at the heart of this is pride. We're afraid of being shown up. We are anxious about comparing unfavourably to other people, other women who seem to have their lives completely sorted; those women in our church who eat the right things, who are never anxious about food; those women in our church who are on diets when they really do not need to be. How do we overcome these thoughts and move from anxiety to freedom?

If you think you're the only woman in your church with anxiety about food, then hear this: you are not.

First we need to recognize that no woman is 'sorted'. No man is sorted, for that matter. No human being is sorted. Each of us comes with our own baggage, faults and insecurities. If you think you're the only woman in your church with anxiety about food, then hear this: you are not. That is what has struck me most in talking to women during the course of writing this book. We think we're alone in this, but we're not. If only we opened up to each other more, we might be able to help each other.

Second, we need to look at what the Bible has to say to us. So many of us are anxious – anxious about our looks, our bodies, how we are perceived, the food that we eat. But 'do not be anxious about *anything*,' (emphasis added) we're told in Philippians 4:6. Do not worry about food. Don't fret about it, don't furrow your brow. Anxiety is not a fruit of the Spirit. As hard as it may be to accept initially, the fact is my anxiety about food displays my lack of faith in a steadfast God in whom I trust and in whom I find my wholeness. I think God knows how hard I find this, to listen to him rather than the accusing and condemnatory voices in my head. That's why the passage in Philippians doesn't end there. It goes on to remind us to talk to God about it – and supernaturally he is able to give us the strength we don't have to overcome our anxieties. Because 'the peace of God, which transcends all understanding, will guard your hearts and your minds in Christ Jesus' (v.7).

Dying to Be Beautiful

For many women, the word 'anxiety' doesn't quite cut it when it comes to describing their relationship with food. For more women than you might think, it's not really about food at all. Eating disorders are dark, obsessive conditions that often have at their root a need to control life's uncertainties by forcing our bodies into submission. I first became aware that there was such a thing as anorexia when, as a young child, I watched *The Karen Carpenter Story*. It's about the beautiful lead singer of the 1970s brother-and-sister pop duo The Carpenters. The film told the story of Karen's rise to stardom, and her secret battle with the eating disorder that eventually led to her death at the age of 32. I

> Today 10 million women in the US battle anorexia and bulimia.

didn't understand it, but the scene with Karen's frail body in the hospital bed haunted my young mind.

Today 10 million women in the US battle anorexia and bulimia. And the numbers worldwide are increasing rather than decreasing. What once was seen as a teenage disease – a phase that many girls go through during puberty – is increasing among women in their 30s, 40s and 50s; often triggered by life events such as having a baby, losing a job, or being bereaved. I came across a study from the University of Edinburgh, carried out in July 2000,[16] of hundreds of teenage girls in rural Ghana and found that some of them had low body weights because of self-imposed diets. Dr Alan Carson, a consultant psychiatrist at the university, said the study 'shows that there may be many reasons why girls develop anorexia and we need to examine this further to see if it goes across cultures and if there is a common approach we can take to tackle it'. Two years later, a study by the University of Zululand in South Africa found that an increasing number of Zulu women were becoming depressed about their weight, and developing eating disorders; using diet pills, laxatives and vomiting their food as a result. Many of them said that they wanted to look less like their own mothers and more like the pictures of Western women they saw in magazines. It shocked and saddened me that women would want to look less like their own mothers. They wanted to deny their heritage and the rich cultural tapestry and genes that made them look the way they did. Because they wanted to look like someone else.

I'm even more shocked as I trawl through stories online of women and young girls whose feelings about their own bodies and the way they look leads to tragedy. Fiona Geraghty, a lively, charming and talented 14-year-old girl from Somerset, UK, killed herself because she thought she was overweight. She hanged herself because she felt she did not look like the girls in the fashion magazines. Rosie Whitaker, 15, jumped in front of a train in Kent after her feelings of being unattractive and overweight led her to suicide and self-harm websites. Ashlynn Conner, an honour roll student from Illinois, US, was just 10 years old when she killed herself after her classmates called her 'fat' and 'ugly'. The list goes on. There are young girls who are literally dying to be beautiful.

Around 80 per cent of 10-year-old boys and girls in America are afraid of being fat. And 43 per cent of first to third graders want to be thinner. In the UK, this increases to 67 per cent among young girls. A report by the Health and Social Care Information Centre in 2012[17] found there had been a 69 per cent increase in the number of girls aged between 10 and 15 who were admitted to hospital for an eating disorder. One in 10 of all the admissions – which overall had increased 16 per cent over the previous 12 months – were 15-year-olds.

> Overweight teenagers and those who believe they are overweight are more likely to have suicidal thoughts.

A study of more than 14,000 high school students in the US in 2009 found that overweight teenagers and those who believe they are overweight are more likely to have suicidal thoughts than those who are not, or those who think they are not.[18] Monica Swahn, who led the study, said: 'Youth feel very pressured to fit in and to fit certain limited ideals of beauty.'

But eating disorders are far more than about a quest to be skinny. Their causes are complex. They are dark. They come from a place of deep soul-pain. They are often a manifestation of a need for control amid life's chaos. They are about existential angst rather than about looking like celebrities. Of all the mental illnesses, eating disorders are responsible for the highest rate of suicide – at around 20 per cent.

Those who have come to a saving faith in Jesus Christ are supposed to be free of the chains that bind us. But so many Christian women are not. We too are suffering from a shattered self-image and we too are suffering from eating disorders. My friend Emma Scrivener has spoken extensively about her battle with anorexia. Like an increasing number of women today, beginning with body dysmorphic thoughts about her weight, she became caught up in a spiral of self-harm that reared its ugly head in the form of a near-fatal eating disorder. I first came across Emma when she spoke at an event I helped to organize – people telling stories of how they found God in a hopeless place. In Emma's case, God saw her through her battle with anorexia.

When I see her speak, I can't help but think how beautiful she is – dark and mysterious, sharing her story in her melodious northern Irish lilt. On the outside, she had no reason to have issues about the way she looked. But we know that looks are deceiving. Inside, she was caught up in a tangled web of control and harmful, addictive behaviours.

'I didn't consider ending my life when I was younger,' she tells me. 'I guess I was doing it in a roundabout way, but that was never my intention. That said, there were times as an adult during recovery, when I felt pretty desperate – though never seriously enough to do anything. And that was in large part because I felt that, even though I was destroying my body, to actually take my own life was a step too far – for God and for the people I loved. But I can understand that people could want to end their lives, because with eating disorders, it's not about just feeling 'fat'. It's about managing emotions and fears – many of which are about life and death and what makes me valuable – not dress size.

'In general I think eating disorders are about trying to make life work rather than seeking death. The difficulty is that what starts as a choice becomes a tyranny – and death is just a side effect. It seems to me that there are two very dangerous times – one is when you've lost a lot of weight and are physically very weak and could well die because of where you're at. On the other side, it's when you're putting weight on – when you lose the coping mechanism that your eating disorder provides – that you start to feel desperate and even suicidal. This is when most sufferers choose to kill themselves – because then you're fighting an addiction on top of all the scary feelings that underpinned it to start with.'

Emma's insight into the mind of anorexia is a real eye-opener for me. If I'm being honest, there were times when I was younger when I wished I had the self-control it takes to have an eating disorder. In my naivety, I saw eating disorders as achieving the elusive 'skinny'. Oh, to be thin. My mind, however, never crossed the line. But so many other minds do, or have done in the past. To try to get a deeper understanding of the anorexic's psyche, I fire up my laptop and type the words 'anorexia tips' into Google. There are more than five million results. I'm stunned. With trepidation, I click on the first entry and am greeted with a whole host of quick and extreme weight loss tips, mantras including 'remember how disgusting fat is' and ideas for dealing with questioning friends and families who show concern about your eating habits. I'm shocked at the kind of information that is readily available in the ether to 'help' people in their disordered eating. Are the media and the Internet to blame? Or would this still exist without them?

> Women were starving themselves long before *Vogue* magazine or Google.

Holy Anorexia

Women were starving themselves long before *Vogue* magazine or Google. And throughout the ages, Christian women's stories have not been any different – in fact, their eating disorder stories have often been intensified; coupled with religious rhetoric and linked with theological doctrine. St Catherine of Siena was a poster girl for holy anorexia.

Born in 1347, she arrived in a medieval world where renouncing the body and putting it under submission were seen as ways of achieving the divine, of meeting with God. When Catherine was 7 years old, she had a vision of Christ. And that's when her disordered eating began. Because that's when she decided to 'deprive herself of this flesh, of all flesh as far as possible'. Though her story is of a different time and a different place, it feels so familiar. When her mother insisted that she eat her food, Catherine started to throw it under the table. From then on she continued to fast, denying her body as a denial of her flesh, but also as penance for sin and guilt. But her extreme eating behaviour was watched with concern, and family members begged her to eat. Don Tommaso of Fonte, the local priest, could not make up his mind about whether Catherine was saintly or whether she was crazy.

In *See Me Naked*,[19] Amy Frykholm explores stories of religious faith and how harmful beliefs about the place of the body can lead to dysfunctional lives. She tells the story of Ashley who, in a bid to subjugate her body and to become perfect, denies herself food.

I came across a number of studies that have found links between religious faith and eating disorders.[20] When I asked around among Christian friends and friends of friends, I found that around 1 in 5 of us have suffered from eating disorders, and a further 1 in 10 were unsure whether or not they had. I used to think eating disorders were things that happened in teenage dramas. I never could have imagined how much it affects so many of the Christian women I know. One told me that the bulimia she suffered from during school and university was 'a convenient way to punish myself for something – probably not being good enough'. Several of the women talked about having to hide their binge eating, gorging on sweets and crisps before making themselves throw it all up again. 'Eating disorders are a way to regain control over your life when you can't control other things,' one former bulimic woman told me. 'They stem from much more than just feeling unattractive.' Saddened as I was to read so many women's stories of battling eating disorders, I was happy they had opened up to me and maybe in some way that could play a part in their healing process. It was however the stories of victory over eating disorders that I found most encouraging. 'I was bulimic as a teenager, but overcame that through God's love for me and his telling me I am beautiful in his sight in my 20s,' one woman shared. Another said: 'I was healed amazingly by coming to an understanding of God's love and grace in my life, and was also hugely supported by outpatient hospital care, which helped me reset a lot of my thought processes and habitual eating/activity behaviour. I believe I may always be susceptible to the thoughts and behaviours I had during that time, but it does not define or control my life like it did.'

The Hungry Soul

Women you know are suffering from anxieties about food – whether that is over-eating or under-eating. Some of these women are suffering in silence, desperately alone. You may be one of these women.

I, too, am one of these women.

My relationship with food wavers between obsessive control and self-discipline, and a complete lack of control – oscillating between over-eating and under-eating. Never just 'eating'. Food and I have a love/hate relationship. I hate myself for loving it. And at various points in my life, I have loved hating it. In the Igbo Nigerian culture that I'm from, food is an integral part of how we do life. I come from a family of food lovers. Food is at the heart of, well, pretty much everything. It is fundamental to how we share community and how we mark rituals – at birthdays, weddings, graduations, funerals and christenings it is the expectation that there will be food and that that food will be provided in abundance. And the food that is provided in abundance is often high in fat and carbohydrates.

It would be easy to put my love of food down to my culture alone. But I think my pre-occupation with food and my lifelong battle with it have been more than about culture. I associate food with happiness. But I also associate it with sadness, loneliness, success, friendship and hospitality. I eat when I'm bored. I eat when I'm stressed. I eat when I'm deliriously happy and I eat when I'm in the depths of despair. I'm obsessed with food. At different stages in my life, this obsession has caused me to pile on the pounds. When you eat in reaction to every single possible human emotion, then you are eating all the time. But I've also had an obsession with not eating at times when I'm in the hallowed 'weight loss zone', which has driven me to lose many pounds.

> I eat when I'm deliriously happy and I eat when I'm in the depths of despair.

I'm not sure when I first became overweight. I look at pictures of myself aged 4 and 5 and I see a skinny, but lanky girl. I have always taken up more space than my female friends. I was always much taller than everybody else and was generally bigger, but I was in proportion for my height. I can pinpoint the moment that changed. One day I was told by a nurse during a health check-up when I was around 13 that I had put on a lot of weight. 'You were lovely and slim before the summer. What happened?' she said. I remember her sending me away with a book about nutrition and body mass index. The years after that were pretty much about me piling on more and more weight. I remember always feeling like my body was betraying me. I felt I didn't eat really badly, so why did I look the way I did?

Looking back, the portions I was eating were huge. I would always have seconds. And, like in many areas of my life, I lacked the ability to say no. My childhood was not average. The 'Ada' (the first daughter) holds a special place in the community of the Igbo tribe. She is well respected and protected within the *umunna* (clan). I have the privilege of being the *ada* of an *ada* of an *ada*. With being the *ada* comes a great sense of responsibility – the *ada* is the second mum of the home. So I found myself preparing food for the family from a very young age. And that meant I was in control of it. I could have as much as I liked. In control of the cooking, but out of control when it came to the craving.

As I grew older, I never, ever weighed myself. The experience of being humiliated in front of the class in primary school scarred me for a very, very long time. It was at university that I reached my heaviest. Still not weighing myself, I had no concept of what I looked like in other people's eyes. My only markers were clothes. I had worn a size 22 dress to my sixth form prom, and that's about where I hovered throughout university. But it was only looking back at photos that I actually saw what I looked like in comparison to everybody else. Those photos made me extremely sad. Ever since I could remember, I had been on various diets. I was one of those who started a diet every Monday; my weight fluctuating – up and down, up and down. I detoxed and I did the Dr Atkins diet; eating steaks and fried eggs for breakfast and all sorts of protein and fat-fuelled meals. They may have been protein and fat-fuelled, but we were told it was all fine, as long as there was not a carb in sight.

I left university and was living the life. With newfound young professional friends, I spent two solid years indulging in the bright lights of London. Most of the friends here were guys so it meant drinking beers and eating late night fried foods. You see, I have never had a problem having friends. I was never bullied or called names because of the way I looked. People liked me. But they just would never have described me as *pretty*. My guy friends wanted me to mother them. My female friends confided in me. I was all things to all friends, desperately people-pleasing so that I would be seen as good, so that I would be valued, beautiful. The London lifestyle all changed when I moved away from the capital to study newspaper journalism on the south coast. Far away from London and away from late nights out with friends, I needed a new challenge. So I joined Weight Watchers.

I can still remember the nausea that swept over me as I waited in line to be weighed at my first meeting. I hadn't been weighed since I was in primary school. I had no idea what the numbers would be. I took off my shoes, held my breath and stepped onto the scale. The number that appeared was far more than I had ever anticipated. I felt sick. I felt embarrassed and overwhelmed with shame. Although I hadn't known what to expect, never in my wildest dreams had I expected that I was that . . . fat.

Despite the hot tears of shame, I will forever be grateful for that moment. Because it spurred me on. It unleashed my competitive streak and unveiled a level of self-control that I had never had. I went jogging early in the morning. I did exercise videos before going to class. I weighed my cereal. I prepared my low-fat lunches. I looked disgustedly at people eating chocolate bars. *Do you know how many points are in those?* And it worked. When I set my mind to something, I want to be the best at it. So each week I was happy that I was losing the most weight; an A-student in slimming. My Weight Watchers leader was impressed that I was the only person who *lost* weight over the Christmas holiday. In the five months that followed, I lost around 60 pounds. And the sense of achievement was heightened by the fact that my clothes got smaller, and my face seemed to emerge from underneath where it had been hiding. People started to compliment me. Men started to ask me out on dates. People started to tell me I was pretty, people started to tell me I was *beautiful.* And I realized no one had really done that before. It felt so good.

Since then, my weight has been something I continue to work on. I go through fad fazes of no carbs, and I feel guilty when I don't go to the gym three times a week. I go through periods of over-eating and periods of cutting back. I am petrified of getting back on the scales one day and seeing the same number that I did that first day of Weight Watchers. Right now I am content in being smaller than I was when I was 18. I'm aware that I have a way to go, not just in terms of reaching the weight and dress size I am supposed to be, but in trying to understand the issues that lie at the heart of my relationship with food.

This is the first time I have ever written about my weight. It is the first time I've talked about these battles. But I have found that so many women struggle with unhealthy relationships with food and I want to be honest about mine. These unhealthy relationships can manifest themselves in eating disorders at either end of the continuum, over-eating and under-eating, or both. They manifest themselves in fad diets, calorie-counting and excessive exercise regimes.

Carol's Story

Carol's weight journey is more extreme than mine, but teaches me a lot about how all these things are tied up in a faulty sense of our true identity. People used to shout abuse at her when she walked down the street. I'm not sure I could have taken that, but Carol tells me she got used to it. She herself only looked in the mirror on very rare occasions, avoiding them at all costs. She even walked along looking at the ground in case she caught sight of her reflection in a window.

'When I looked in the mirror, what I saw was so utterly appalling.'

'When I looked in the mirror, what I saw was so utterly appalling that it reinforced the negative perceptions of self that I got from other people,' Carol tells me. She had always been heavy and had become accustomed to being judged before being known. She recalls going for an interview for a job at a Christian organization – a job that she was well qualified for. 'I have no doubt that I didn't get that job because of what I looked like,' she says. 'As soon as the interviewer looked at me, I saw him make judgments about me. People look not on the heart but on your outward appearance – and that's also definitely true within the church.

'If you're a Christian, the perception is that you ought to be able to sort this junk out,' she says. 'You ought to be able to live better. And the older I got and the heavier I got, those pressures increased. How could I stand up with any integrity in front of a group of people and talk about the life-transforming power of Jesus when I looked the way I did? There were also people who cheerfully told me that self-control was one of the fruits of the Spirit. It added a whole new level of pressure.'

At the age of 49, she had had enough of being looked at in the street and judged in church. So she undertook a dramatic food replacement diet. Drinking two shakes a day, she lost 140 pounds in 10 months. And with her significant weight loss came a dramatic change in her life. Abuse was no longer hurled at her when she walked down the street. Her doctors were happy. And in church, she received a lot of affirmation. Her church family told her she looked great. 'I was totally believing at that point that the whole thing was over with.'

But it was not.

Because over the next year, she regained the weight she had lost – and then some. Around 154 pounds. As the weight crept back on, the compliments dried up. I know just what she was experiencing at this point. When I lose a significant amount of weight, I become addicted to the compliments I get week after week as the pounds drop off and people's eyes widen in amazement when they see me.

As Carol returned to her former self, the church friends who had been giving her affirmation no longer knew what to say to her. 'There is no more visible failure than someone who loses a considerable amount of weight and then puts it back on,' Carol says. 'So I pretty much quit on life. I stopped going to church. I cut most of my friends and family out of my life because it was too painful to have to keep explaining what was happening. I had regained the weight because I was still exactly the same person on the inside. The huge problem with the diet philosophy is that you're always thinking about food, or weighing it out or thinking about the next carrot stick or whatever it is. But by definition, diets only change what's on the outside. They don't address all the complex issues which led to it in the first place.'

> 'I found my total identity was absolutely in crisis – it was fracturing.'

Carol had hit rock bottom and decided to make an even more drastic decision. After looking into surgical options, she had a gastric bypass in May 2009. Very soon she had the body she had always dreamed of. Everything was in proportion. She could wear size 10 trousers, but still something was not right.

'I found my total identity was absolutely in crisis – it was fracturing,' she remembers. 'All of my reasonably conscious life my identity had been so rooted in being a fat person that when that was taken away, I no longer had a frame of reference for who I was.'

Carol's dramatic weight loss led to some bizarre experiences, which she shares with me, my mouth agape. In a bid to lose weight even more rapidly, she under-ate after the bypass. And because this meant her nutrition was so bad, her hair fell out and she had to wear a wig. On occasion, she found that people she had known for years would walk past her in the street. One day she turned up at church and was asked by someone who had been her friend for 10 years: 'Is it your first time?' 'It was totally dislocating,' she tells me. 'I felt I'd lost all kinds of context for life. When I looked in the mirror when I was losing all the weight, I was still seeing a fat person. For the first time I was able to understand how anorexics can look in the mirror and be presented with a distorted view of themselves. It was very hard for me to replace the image that was burned onto my brain with the new one. I even carried around a photo of my old self as a terrible warning.'

She spoke to someone at church about it, but Christians didn't really know what to say. She was told just to get her thinking right and make '47 faith confessions before breakfast' and it would all be OK. No one tried to find out the root cause of her disordered eating. She eventually found freedom not in weight loss, or compliments, but in Christ.

While attending a Beauty for Ashes retreat,[21] her eyes were opened to the deeper issues that had led to her over-eating and her emptiness even after the weight had gone. 'I had not grasped what it meant for God to lavish his love on me,' she says. 'A significant turning point in my journey to healing was coming into an encounter with Jesus and asking him to change my name. I asked him to give me the name that reflected how he saw me – and that was "Heaven's Joy and Delight". He showed me that my name was written on the palm of his hand.

'The more I travel on this journey, the more I realize that none of this is actually about physical beauty. It's about understanding uncondi-tional love, and about understanding how to receive this unconditional love. Because to receive unconditional love, it's first necessary to believe oneself loveable. And for so many people, that's where it falls over.'

The Alabaster Jar

She wipes his feet with her hair.

This woman, the dirty, sinful, ill-mannered woman. She bursts onto the scene where Jesus is having a respectable dinner with one of the Pharisees. Unannounced, she enters armed only with an alabaster box of ointment. She knows that he knows the things that she has done – the bad things. She knows that he knows the thoughts she has had about others, about herself. She knows he can see she doesn't think she's worth anything. But she knows that all she wants to do, right in that moment, in that place, is pour everything out to him in total, unashamed, absolute devotion. Nothing else matters in that moment, in that place. It's all about this Jesus. The Christ. God in human form.

And she does all she can think to do. She weeps. Washing his feet with her tears. And she wipes them with her hair – her crowning glory; laying her beauty and her identity, all that she is, down at his feet. And she kisses them and anoints them with the ointment from her alabaster jar. And though she pours out her devotion to him, she's afraid that he will reject her just like everyone else has. She wonders whether she will be kicked out, proved worthless; tossed out like a rag. But then she hears him speak.

She hears him talk to Simon. 'See this woman?' he says. 'See what she's done? I came into your house and you didn't give me anything – not a drop of water to wash my feet. But she has wet my feet with her tears. She's wiped them with her hair.'

And she can't breathe. She's wondering how this will play out.

Then he says to her that the bad things she's done are forgiven. And he says to her that her faith has saved her. 'Go in peace,' he says.

I love this story. I love that Jesus accepts this scandalous woman, who is never truly seen by the society in which she lives. He knows that she's not perfect, but it really doesn't matter. It's her devotion to him that he wants because he knows that that's what will make her whole again. As UK theologians Tidball and Tidball write: 'He singles her out as a model of faith and of the way God longs to furnish women with his *shalom* however corrupted God's image had become within them.'[22]

I love that she wipes his feet with her hair. Her hair is not her priority. It's no longer in her hair that she finds her identity. She wants to rid herself of the label: the prostitute with the long hair symbolizing the looser morals. She is willing to let it all go. She knows that she has to if she is ever to find wholeness.

It's amazing to think that it's her total abandon, her freedom to honour Christ with her whole body, that helps her to find the ultimate freedom in him.

What does freedom mean? It means the absence of any hindrance or restraint. So what are the things that hinder me from saying and believing that I am beautiful? Society's narrow definition of what beautiful is, my negative thought patterns and behaviours, a failure to remember – or be aware of – what God says about me, and therefore an inaccurate perception that I am not of value, that I'm not accepted, that I'm not loved and that I am not good enough. In Christ we can be free from all of this. In him, we are no longer slaves to the society in which we live; we are free from those painful thoughts that come into our heads, we are free to believe that in him we are . . . good. Because of our relationship with God, where there once was a need to control and punish our unwieldy bodies to achieve beauty, we are free to *be* beautiful. We're free to revel in his total acceptance of us, including our bodies, just as we are. 'Therefore, there is now no condemnation for those who are in Christ Jesus' (Rom. 8:1). We're free from condemnation, both from the world in which we live, and from the thoughts that inhabit our heads.

> The path to freedom isn't always instant.

The path to freedom isn't always instant, and often we need to be reminded that we have been freed. Each step along the way we need the help of the Holy Spirit, guiding us and walking with us and renewing our minds so that we can see the truth about who we are, and find peace in that.

A pre-occupation with ourselves, and any feelings of inadequacy we have, also hinders us from moving on. We – you and I – are amazing, talented, beautiful women with so much potential to be justice-seekers and peace-makers. We need to find freedom in Christ to be able to go forward, totally abandoned to what God would have us do. Our freedom is for a purpose.

Prayer

Dear life-giving God,

Thank you that you have already freed me. I will forever praise you because I am no longer a slave to anything – not unhealthy thoughts or eating habits, not a negative sense of my body or myself. Free from hating my body and free to see it as fearfully and wonderfully made. I pray that your Holy Spirit will help me understand my freedom as a living, breathing truth so that I may walk tall in that freedom. I pray that freedom too for my sisters in the church – those who I walk alongside. Help us to embrace the freedom that you have given us. Help us to know that we are beautiful. And help us to see that same beauty in others, in the world around us. Help us to love ourselves, love others and bring your wholeness and peace to the brokenness around us.

Amen

Questions to Ponder

- Make a list of all the different ways you control what you look like. Does the list surprise you?
- How would you describe your relationship with food?
- Are the media and fashion industries to blame for the rise in eating disorders?

- Have you ever experienced similar attitudes to those shown by Carol's church when she put all the weight back on? How do you think churches, and individuals, should respond?
- Galatians 5:1 says that we've been totally set free and that we're no longer to be slaves to anything. What does that look like practically when we think about ourselves as slaves to our beauty regimes?

Beauty Challenge

Calculate how much you have spent on 'beautification' in the past month and give that same amount away to the work of a charity that's close to your heart.

5.

Enemies of Beauty

Am I beautiful? There are forces that conspire against us believing that we are; things that rear their ugly heads and get in the way – joy stealers like jealousy, comparison, low self-esteem and shame, as well as a desperate need for affirmation from all the wrong places. These are things we project outwards and they all act as barriers against finding that eternal sense that we are worthy, valuable, good, beautiful.
That can only come from one place.

'We ask ourselves, who am I to be brilliant, gorgeous, talented, fabulous? Actually, who are you not to be? You are a child of God. Your playing small does not serve the world.' (Marianne Williamson)

'No one can make you feel inferior without your consent.'
(Eleanor Roosevelt)

Comparison Culture

Earlier, I shared with you my realization, aged 5, that I didn't look like all the other little girls in my class. I guess what lay behind the revelation was a feeling of not measuring up to everyone else. Well this has resulted in a niggling obsession with comparing myself to the people around me constantly. Sometimes I find that I'm that same 5-year-old girl looking around at what other people have got and seeing whether or not I can equal that – or if I fall short.

> We exist in a culture that sees everything through the prism of comparison.

We exist in a culture that sees everything through the prism of comparison. Our achievements, our successes and our happiness are often judged not in isolation, not in and of themselves, but compared to others' achievements, their successes and their happiness.

Let me ask you something. Would you rather earn £100,000 a year when your friends' average salary is £200,000 a year? Or would you rather earn £50,000 when they earn on average a salary of £25,000 a year? As great as it would be to earn that £100,000 salary, in reality, we judge our salaries not in and of themselves, but how they measure up against everyone else's around us. We don't mind earning less, as long as we are earning more than other people.

We live in a comparison culture. But imagine how much happier you would be if you couldn't compare yourselves to others. If your salary, your family, your car, your clothes, the hours you give to church, your job, your Twitter following, your relationship status were just so. Judged not in comparison to others, but just . . . so. Imagine what a difference it could make if we were free of this need to compare.

I recently met up with a group of female Christian leaders. Around 50 of us gathered from all over the country to hang out with each other, to network, to learn from each other. But this was no ordinary meeting of women. In our first session, we were asked to discuss why it is that women hate each other, why it is that all-female meetings such as the one we were sitting in filled so many of us with dread.

One by one we shared our feelings, our dread at the prospect of being in a room full of women. We realized that these feelings were stirred up in us because women are often pitted against each other, compared to each other, in competition with each other. We compete to be the most beautiful, the perfect wife, the best boss, the most successful, the best dressed, the best cook, the smartest, the best mother.

I've realized that, for me, comparison is a huge issue. One with which I have always battled. I tie myself up in knots comparing myself to other people, and this has some pretty ugly side effects such as competition and jealousy. And it's other women that my obsessive comparison disorder is focused on, most of the time. Because being a woman is the part of my identity that I ascribe to the most.

When I compare myself with others, then I am most likely to compare myself with other women. Brené Brown explains that that's because we often feel the need to compare ourselves with people similar to us or people in situations similar to our own. Our mantra is: 'Be just like everyone else, but better.'[23]

We see comparison everywhere. For example, the underlying ethos of today's entertainment industry seems to be compare and compete. There are endless seasons of shows such as *The X Factor*, *American Idol*, *Big Brother* and *Four Weddings*, which ask the audience to compare each of the candidates and to vote for their favourites. The candidates themselves can't be too wacky as they will be voted off or lose; but yet they need to stand out, and need to be better than the people they're competing with.

I am always comparing myself to others. If you're a friend of mine, then I've probably compared myself to you. I have taken mental note of whether people are skinnier than me, or fatter than me. How my thighs and belly compare to theirs. Whether they look good in a strapless dress; whether they are the perfect height to carry off stilettos. I've judged people on whether they have better skin than me and been jealous of them if they have. Do they have better hair? Better teeth? Do they have a boyfriend? Do they drive a better car? Own a bigger flat? Are they a better public speaker? How many books have they written? Are they married? Do they have children? Are they more beautiful?

When I spend energy seeing how I measure up to other people, then more often than not, I find myself wanting, failing. It's a constant drain of disappointment and it hurts.

> When I spend energy seeing how I measure up to other people . . . it's a constant drain of disappointment and it hurts.'

It seems that I'm not the only one that is obsessively comparative. In the conversations I've had over the past few months with women, it is something that shows up time and time again. Often we find that our sense of our own beauty, our value and self-worth is measured in relation to others. I found that 75 per cent of us feel jealous about another woman's appearance either occasionally or often. Around 6 per cent of us say we feel constant jealousy towards other women's looks.

My life so far has included periods of great weight loss and great weight gain. When I'm in 'the zone' you will not see a carbohydrate or a chocolate bar pass my lips. During these periods of intense dieting, exercise, food paranoia and obsession, I thrive on compliments from others as they watch the pounds drop off. As these pounds melt away, I get more compliments because I also make more effort. I do my hair better. I spend more time on my make-up and will buy new clothes to fit my new frame. My friends and family notice the change and I absolutely love the thrill that it gives me when they see my transformation. Their words make me feel admired, valued, beautiful.

This is a good thing.

But it's also a bad thing.

I'm going to tell you a story I'm ashamed of. Following one period of quite successful weight loss, a friend of mine started to follow the plan that I had been on. As I began eating more freely after having lost some weight, she was becoming stricter with her eating regime – as I had been only a short while before. But as the pounds fell of her, instead of being an encourager and telling her about how beautiful she was, I became jealous. Ridiculously so. Every time I saw her she looked smaller. Every time someone gave her a compliment about her having lost weight, I felt jealous pangs the likes of which I had not felt before. The feeling was so intense that I found myself incapable of giving her any compliments whatsoever. I pretended not to notice her weight loss. Feigning ignorance, I carried on as normal while other friends would tell her how great she looked.

I could not give my friend the words that she needed to hear because I was jealous, full of insecurity and ultimately full of pride. My pride had been dented. I had delighted in the words of encouragement that I had received when I had been the one losing all the weight. But, really, I wasn't feeling beauty in and of itself. I just felt more beautiful than my previous self and more beautiful than others who hadn't been on this weight loss journey. When someone else started to go through the same process, I felt completely threatened. Something ugly inside me couldn't bear the thought of sharing the throne that I had mistakenly thought I sat on. Ultimately my sense of beauty had depended on a comparison with others. When someone else started to be praised for being beautiful, my pride was deflated.

This kind of hostility and resentment should have no place within the church and the Kingdom of God. These are enemies that seek to destroy the amazing strength that could be created in the bond of sisterhood. It renders us foes, forever thinking negatively of each other, rather than being allies in the justice-fighting and the peace-making. Re-telling the story of my jealousy makes me desperately sad. I would hate anyone to have those kinds of thoughts about me. Because I think I'm overall a pretty good person. But when I ponder my thoughts about other people – my friends – I'm totally ashamed. My friend Hannah recently challenged a group of women at our church. She asked us whether we would be as happy for someone else succeeding – getting married, winning an award, writing a book, losing weight, getting a great job – as we would be if it were us succeeding. And bang, it hit me. I realized the extent of my jealousy, competition and comparison; my feeling suffocated by others' success as if it somehow takes away from my own. But beauty is not a zero-sum game. Someone else being beautiful does not make me any less so. There's room enough for all of us.

> Someone else being beautiful does not make me any less so.

Jesus challenges us to love our neighbours as ourselves. But I'm not sure I have really done this. I love my friends, but I really want to get to a place where I love them in that radical way that Jesus calls us to love. Completely, honestly and fully. I want to love them so much that I am genuinely their biggest fan; cheering them on for every success, every good thing in their lives, as if it were my own. Loving them so much that there is no room for jealousy, no ugly need to better their success, no tiresome drive to outdo them or to dismiss the good things in their lives. I want to really love them; to tell them that in every area of their lives they really are beautiful.

I really want this to become a living truth in the way I live my life. But it seems there is an enemy who just won't let it be so. All my striving, my jealousy, comparison and rivalry are driven by some unconscious desperation to boost my own ego and self-esteem.

Desperately Seeking Self-esteem

I have returned to Cambridge University where I was an undergraduate. As I sit writing in the world-famous University Library, old, wise books surround me; I sit among some of the brightest brains in the world. It's all coming back to me – these feelings of familiarity and love for my alma mater. But they are accompanied by my old friends: anxiety, pressure, comparison and competition. The nauseating stomach churn of the drive to be the best.

I do love this place; this bastion of academia, its cobbled streets where the likes of Samuel Taylor Coleridge, Sylvia Plath and John Milton walked, learnt and grew. A place of learning where intelligence is the virtue to be celebrated, where excellence is rewarded.

I'm back here for a lavish ten-year dinner that my college at the university has put on for us – a reunion to celebrate a decade since we were dropped off by our parents, wide-eyed and ready to start three years of study.

I was surrounded by women who had what we all yearn for: brains and beauty.

Back in this place, I am overcome with nostalgia. Really, these were the best of times. But they were also the worst of times, where my self-esteem was most affected. Physically, I reached my heaviest, piling on the pounds that accompanied this quaint university life of three-course formal dinners, drinking societies and late-night pizzas in the offices of the university newspaper.

As I wander through my old haunts in this beautiful city, I can't help but smile at the old times. But I also realize that, physically, I was desperately unhappy. I was surrounded by women who had what we all yearn for: brains and beauty. I felt like I came up lacking on both fronts. And there's one thing that reminds me of this more clearly than any other that, though this was a place of academia, intelligent women were still rated on whether they were hot or not.

It's the wall that stood behind the bar at my college.

The wall was lined with passport photos of female students the barmen felt were pretty enough to be put on display. The wall was covered with the beautiful faces of these female Cambridge undergraduates. These women who had worked hard to get to the university, but then who willingly offered themselves up as objects to be ogled.

It didn't seem like a big deal at the time. This Celebration of Hotness seemed perfectly fine and normal – just a part of university life. But, thinking back, I remember a small sinking feeling every time I ordered a drink at that bar. Because I never made it onto that wall. My university days were probably the height of my unhappiness with my body – and the height of my body weight. When I think back to that wall, an overwhelming feeling of inadequacy comes rushing back to me. While I focused on working hard to get the best essay results I could, and worked tirelessly on the university paper, I would have loved to have been asked for my photo for that wall of fame. Just to have been asked. Of course I would have declined . . .

But no one ever asked me for my photo. Although I was well liked, I was the 'nice one' throughout school. I was everyone's friend, but I longed to be affirmed in the way I looked, not just my personality or my academic ability. If you had asked me whether I would pick brains or beauty – I would have chosen beauty. No doubt about it.

Would my self-esteem have been any better during my university days if I had made it onto that wall? Who knows? But I was desperately seeking self-esteem and thought that my face on that wall was my ticket to it.

So many of us seem to wear low self-esteem as a badge – a reason why we feel bad about ourselves. Low self-esteem, the plight of womankind. It's why so many of us flock to the self-help aisles in book stores, frantically in search of it. We're desperately seeking magic solutions to the way we feel about ourselves. It's hardly a surprise then that in the UK, while book sales overall were down during the economic downturn, the sales of self-help books have rocketed 25 per cent. In the US, the self-help market is worth an estimated $10 billion a year.[24]

There is something paradoxical about being obsessed with boosting our self-esteem. Maybe low self-esteem is actually about having too high a view of myself in the first place. Why do I strive to boost my self-esteem, to believe that I am the prettiest, the cleverest, the kindest, the most accomplished? And why is it so painful when I realize that I'm not. Is low self-esteem actually in essence about my pride? Why do I ask whether I am beautiful? Maybe even asking the question is a symptom of my self-centeredness. Even the thought makes me feel ashamed.

I decided to speak to Jennie Frost, to ask her opinion on whether my low self-esteem is really all about my ego. Jennie set up Beauty Cocoon in 2011 because she had come across a lot of people – especially young women – who had very low views of themselves. Passionate about seeing young women feel valued and find purpose in their lives, she set about creating resources to boost their self-esteem.

'I very much see self-esteem as our view of ourselves, our ability to make decisions and deal with circumstances in life,' Jennie tells me. 'Rather than a focus on ourselves in an egotistical manner it is more about having a realistic view of ourselves, our interests, personalities, but also the things we don't enjoy or are not as good at.

'Positive self-esteem is integral to us being contributing members of society and from a faith perspective affects the way we interact with others and with God. When we look at self-esteem as Christians, it is always in the context of being loved and valued by God. But he loves us for who we are and I think there is freedom in getting to know ourselves.'

He loves us for who we are. Loved and valued by God. Statements like this feel like they could be found in those self-esteem-boosting self-help books. But when I dwell on these statements, I'm reminded again of their truth. They haven't come from nowhere, plucked out of thin air to make me feel good about myself. They find their origin in God-breathed biblical statements.

When I read in 1 John 3:1 that I'm a child of God, it makes me feel accepted. When I read in Ephesians 2:10 that I'm God's 'handiwork', it makes me feel special. When I read in Luke 12:7 that the hairs on my head are numbered, it makes me feel important. When I read in Isaiah 43:4 that I'm 'precious' in God's eyes, it makes me feel beautiful.

> Christ came so that we might be free.

It's amazing to remember that there is someone who is able to empower us and to make us feel that we are of worth. And he wants to be in relationship with us. He longs for us to look to him for guidance. He longs for us to seek him in everything that we do. He longs to be involved in every area of our lives – even the things we think are mundane. 'For the LORD your God goes with you; he will never leave you nor forsake you' (Deut. 31:6). He also wants to free us from all the negative trappings associated with our humanity. Christ came so that we might be free. Free indeed. And that means free from everything. All the rubbish. All the hurt. All the feelings of inadequacy.

Over and over and over again, Scripture reminds me that I am loved and valued by a Father God who thinks I am worth something. Not because I'm clever, not because I'm kind and certainly not because my face makes its way onto a hotness wall in a student bar.

Armed with that knowledge, I am free to understand who I am and who I was made to be. Armed with that knowledge, I can bat away those enemies of jealousy, comparison and low self-esteem, that whisper lies to me.

Beneath the Surface: What's Going On?

Do you have a girlfriend who insists on putting herself down? On a night out, you compliment her on her new dress. 'You look great in that,' you say, giving her a warm smile. And she shrugs, pouts and says: 'Oh, this? I feel really fat in it. Look at my huge belly and my bum looks awful in it. I'm not sure the colour suits me.' You feel like asking: 'Well, why did you buy it then?' but instead you reassure her and say again: 'You look amazing. Really.'

Or picture the scene: you are looking through Facebook photos of a big night out that you and your close friends recently had. And up pops a message from a girlfriend, who says: 'I look awful in those photos! Detag! Detag!' And you can't see it. She looks as lovely as ever.

So what's really going on here? When a girlfriend looks amazing, but she insists she doesn't; when you compliment her but she bats those words away like she's swatting away flies. Maybe she genuinely feels that she looks awful. Maybe it's a feeling she lives with every day, which is why when you tell her she looks great, she is incapable of believing you. But what on earth could make this beautiful woman feel awful every single day of her life?

Did her dad tell her she was beautiful when she was a little girl?

Did boys at school tell her that she was not?

Does she feel inadequate when looking around at the women in her life, comparing herself to them?

Or does she constantly compare herself to women in magazines and television shows and every single time find herself lacking?

There could be another reason. When she's putting herself down, is she just wanting a bit of attention, a dose of affirmation? I know I've done it. When you put yourself down, you're hoping that others will protest because you think that in some way this will help boost your self-esteem. When I make statements about how ugly I am, or how fat

I look in that dress, maybe I'm desperately crying out for someone to affirm me, to tell me that I am beautiful.

Because when I ask *Am I Beautiful?*, in a search for self-esteem, I am not just asking whether I am pretty, whether I have a face that could launch a thousand ships, whether I look good in my jeans. I am asking whether I am valuable. Whether I am accepted. Whether I am good. Whether I am loved.

All About Eve

Let's just think about Eve's self-esteem for a moment. There she was, before the Fall, the crown of creation. The first and only woman. Hanging out with God and Adam. Being lavished with love by both. I'm guessing she would have felt pretty good about herself. She had no mirrors, no magazines, no supermodels, no model friends, to compare herself to. She didn't face the pressures that the modern woman faces, constantly. She couldn't envy her girlfriend's thick hair or wish she had J-Lo's bum. She couldn't compare herself to Halle Berry or Giselle because she was pretty much it. Quite literally a super model. We today on the other hand are constantly exposed to these images of stunningly beautiful women each and every day of our lives, on the television, in magazines, on billboards, on the Internet. In fact it's estimated that we see between 400 and 600 images of women in advertising each day.[25]

In *The Whole Woman*, Germaine Greer writes: 'Every woman knows that, regardless of all her other achievements, she is a failure if she is not beautiful.'[26]

Beauty is the standard by which women are judged. It is a marker of the elusive 'complete package'. Healthy, wealthy, brainy, successful, kind, beautiful. I'm not happy about this. I'm not sure that's what God wants for us. This dissatisfaction. This feeling of un-prettiness. This low self-esteem. This body hatred. I think he'd like us to feel our bodies are beautiful. And I think that we need all the help we can get in our quest to feel beautiful.

We can help ourselves, too, using Eve as our example. We can make more of an effort to see ourselves as individuals existing in relationship with God, not looking around at other women and measuring ourselves against them, but focusing on walking with God. The more we walk with him, the more we will know how valued and loved we are, how beautiful we are, because we are so precious to him.

> The more we walk with him, the more we will know how valued and loved we are.

Seeking Affirmation

I was sitting in a tube carriage on my way home from work. I wasn't looking or feeling my best. It had been a hard day, but I didn't care. As I scanned the carriage, I saw a beautiful blonde; her hair effortlessly tussled over her shoulders, her red heels adding a dash of colour to her skirt suit. Just before the train pulled into Bank station, she rose and tottered down the aisle, squeezing herself through gaps under men willingly offering their armpits as archways for her to glide through. Until she was gone. But I kept watching the men in the carriage, their eyes gawping at her, long after she was off the platform.

Men just can't seem to help themselves. I watch them. I watch them watching beautiful women. I've formed a habit of tracking the direction of men's eyes when a good-looking woman walks past them. It's humorous in its predictability. And it makes me angry. How dare they objectify women in this way? How dare they feel they have the right to stare at a woman like she is a walking rib-eye steak? This is the strong-independent-woman-me talking. The one who feels she must defend womankind and fight back against this shallowness of mankind.

But strong-independent-woman-me is shouting so loud because she's trying to suppress the voice of the real me. The one who hopes longingly – despite her protestations – that men will look at *her*. The one who is desperately seeking to satisfy that inner craving that she be aligned with beauty. She hopes, but doesn't shout too loudly, that men's eye lines will follow her footsteps as she walks past them. She hopes that they will want to linger a moment longer on her elegant frame. She longs for them to find her beautiful.

My mother says there is really only one person she wants to think her beautiful – and that's my father. She tells me that, although everyone would like the world to consider them pretty, one man thinking that you are the most beautiful, that you are enough, is all a woman needs. Who can deny the power of a man who you love telling you how beautiful you are? And some men are great at letting the women in their lives know this.

Women crave that attention, affirmation and validation from the men they are in relationships with. We all love to be told we're beautiful, but some women purposefully seek out a man because he makes them feel fabulous. They can get so wrapped up in the fawning and the constant stream of compliments that they feel lost and confused when that stops.

When we seek validation from a man who tells us we are beautiful, then that can have dangerous consequences. We feel good about ourselves for a moment. But soon afterwards we crave more – more fawning and mollycoddling and complimenting. What happens if he stops telling you that you're beautiful? What if another man makes you feel even more beautiful?

Our society is one in which so often women find their worth in the way they look. The assumption is that if they look their best they will be able to find a good man, who will look after them and tame the insecurities they have about the way they look. And it's a society that cheers women on to find someone who makes them feel beautiful. The need to feel beautiful trumps many other needs that make for a successful relationship. But we run into problems when being told that we are beautiful gives us validation, and when not being told we are beautiful in some way devalues us. If the more praise and compliments we receive, the more validated and valued we feel, then something is very wrong.

One woman told me: 'I started looking online for my self-worth from men – from older men who would tell me how beautiful I was and how much prettier than their wives or girlfriends, and it got really graphic. I felt disgusted with myself, but when it came to being in a relationship myself, and my partner would tell me I was beautiful, I'd always have in my head: "Yeah, but who else are you saying that to?" It's become an addiction that plagues me every day.'

When I read this woman's story, I was shocked but at the same time unsurprised; because I know how easy it can be to become addicted to compliments and how those compliments can fill a temporary hole. As flawed human beings we are constantly craving affirmation and validation – from anywhere we can get it. We could momentarily find validation in older men online, our husbands telling us we are the most beautiful woman in the world, being told 'well done' at work, in someone saying the meal we cooked was delicious, or having our name on the cover of a book.

> We are trying to find our eternal value in things that are here for a moment.

So often, I get my sense of value and worth from my family, from the number of friends I have, from the number of people who like me, from how full my diary is, from the number of Twitter followers I have, the number of Facebook friends I gather, the number of Google hits to my name, the amount of money I have in my bank account, how I look. Some of these are good things. But, like this world, all are fleeting. We are trying to find our eternal value in things that are here for a moment. The prophet Jeremiah warns of the dangers of looking to humans instead of God, but points to what reward there is when God is the focus: 'Cursed are those who put their trust in mere humans, who rely on human strength and turn their hearts away from the LORD . . . But blessed are those who trust in the LORD, and have made the LORD their hope and confidence' (Jer. 17:5–10, NLT). And when we do this – look to humans instead of God – we will constantly be disappointed. Life will continue to be a rollercoaster of seeking, finding and losing validation.

One friend shared with me how she has managed to get the perspective right: 'As a married woman, I don't feel my confidence/self-esteem/value/beauty are dependent on my husband's compliments, which is a good job as his main way of being loving is to do jobs for me. Having previously been married to a horrifically abusive man, I know the significance of the way in which words can devalue and damage a person. However, my value is no longer dependent on external views of me, whether my husband or anyone compliments me, but on the truth that I am valued by He Who Is.'

But, for many, this craving for beauty seems never-ending. As a child, I wanted to wear make-up. As a 20-something singleton, I feel I have to make an effort to be as beautiful as possible so that I can catch a man (before obviously letting him get to know the 'me' that lies beneath the exterior). The Christian sub-culture sends conflicting messages when it comes to the search for a hubby. Yeah, sure, we know it's what's on the inside that counts and that we are supposed to prepare our character, become the best that we can be inside, before we are matched with our 'life partner'. We know that charm is deceitful and beauty is vain. But we don't see very many Christian men praying for a plain wife. We are told that men are visual beings – even Christian men – so we want to do our utmost to reel one in with our physical attractiveness.

I'm aware here that I may be making assumptions about mankind. So I decided to look for a guy's opinion. Barry Cooper is the face of the *Christianity Explored* discipleship videos. In a blog he says: 'The pornography epidemic raises – or rather, lowers – the bar on what we expect of a prospective spouse because of its unremitting insistence on physical performance and cosmetic beauty, over and against mental and moral qualities. As Christian men, we may pray unctuously for the Lord to provide a wife of noble character, but our hearts are being continually conditioned to lust after the wife of maximal hotness. "Charm is deceitful," God protests, "and beauty is vain!" But we dismiss him like one of those impertinent pop-ups that gets in the way of what we really want to see.'[27]

Proverbs 31 woman, you rock. I'd love to be you. But being you alone isn't going to bag me a husband, I believe. So I fall into the trap of thinking that I just need to keep up the beauty thing until I find a husband. Because surely it doesn't matter afterwards. He's in the bag, right? I am free to let my inner Proverbs 31 shine. But then I think of that clichéd line we see in films and on advertising billboards – a woman asking the man in her life: 'Does my bum look big in this?' The woman who still craves affirmation from the one who loves her. She wants her man to tell her that she is beautiful, that her bum looks great even if it looks big, that he loves her just the way she is.

I've heard some of my married friends let slip some of the pressures they feel to be 'hot and holy' for their husbands. And often churches do not help in this regard, giving the impression that looking beautiful is a woman's duty; something that pleases her husband and ensures that his eyes do not stray to another whom he judges more beautiful.

There is nothing wrong with looking beautiful and pleasing your husband, if doing so also makes you feel good, of value and of worth. But the suggestion underlying this is that being attractive is the priority for a Christian wife. It is not. For both the husband and the wife, the priority must be loving God and loving each other as they love themselves.

But some people seem to forget this. In 2006, it was revealed that celebrity Christian Ted Haggard had been in a homosexual affair.

Controversial US pastor Mark Driscoll responded with the following: 'It is not uncommon to meet pastors' wives who really let themselves go; they sometimes feel that because their husband is a pastor, he is therefore trapped into fidelity, which gives them cause for laziness. A wife who lets herself go and is not sexually available to her husband in the ways that Song of Songs is so frank about is not responsible for her husband's sin, but she may not be helping him either.'[28]

A wife who lets herself go? What does that mean? A wife who lets herself relax, who does not obsess over her beauty regime and diet, who chooses to go natural instead of caking her face in make-up? Comments like this add to the pressure on women to control their unwieldy bodies, to keep them in check lest the man in their lives no longer finds them attractive and is therefore given permission to find some other beauty. Until she too lets herself go. The comments are also unfair to men and assumes that – though they have taken a vow of commitment to their wife, for better or worse, for fatter or thinner, for younger or older – they will feel the need to leave if their wife no longer looks the way she did on their wedding day.

Though we might blame society and Christian leaders like Driscoll for making women feel their identity is found in how they look, it seems that women all over the world do themselves really long to be thought of as beautiful; to be adored by men. There's something about a man telling you that he thinks you are pretty/gorgeous/hot/beautiful. It's these adjectives that can stir something in us in a way that being described as intelligent/caring/funny often cannot.

I want to be all these things. Yes, I really do want men to think I'm intelligent with a great sense of humour. I want them to find me witty, charming, fun to be with. But alongside these things, I hope that they will also find me beautiful. Because when you're beautiful, the world seems to let you get away with not being intelligent. When you're beautiful, you can get away with not being very nice. When you're beautiful, no one cares whether or not you're funny. When you're beautiful you are valued, you are prized, you are accepted and you are good.

I have recently taken to asking my guy friends to tell me, honestly, what it is about men and their obsession with beautiful women. They pretty much all tell me that it's not about beautiful women. It's about women full stop. They love women. They love the female form. Maybe they were designed that way. They think women are beautiful in a way that men can never be. They are drawn to a woman's beauty, but it's far more than about her dress size or the colour of her hair. Kindness is beautiful. A gentle spirit is beautiful. Someone who supports and encourages them, makes them laugh, understands them, is beautiful.

Kindness is beautiful. A gentle spirit is beautiful.

I asked some of my male friends to tell me the top five attributes that they look for, or had looked for, in a wife. I was sure that 'beautiful' or 'hot' would make its way into the top five on most occasions. I got a whole range of answers: from 'shared faith', 'creativity', 'good at dancing', 'knows her own mind' to 'being a fan of *Doctor Who*' and 'knowing the rules of cricket'. Guys wanted 'strength of character' and someone who would 'put up' with them. They were looking for someone who was compatible with them, who they could grow old and not grow bored with. I was surprised at how few of them made reference to physical attributes. For them attraction was about the whole package.

I had expected them to allude in some way to physical attractiveness, even if they meant it in a broad sense. But most of them didn't. And that was a relief; freeing me to concentrate on being the truest 'me' that I can be, developing my character and focusing on the great things about me as a person. Freedom comes in that rather than squeezing into a certain dress size.

Daddy's Girl

I'm a daddy's girl. I think my dad is the greatest man ever to have lived. When I think back on the proudest moments of my life, the news of them has been followed by an immediate longing to tell my dad. That's the first thing I'll do – pick up the phone and call him. Because I know that he is often more proud of me than I am of myself. I love his approval. I love hearing the words: 'I'm proud of you.' There's nothing like it. I've loved hearing his approval ever since I was a little girl. The beam on his face has always been the same, whether it's been at me saying my first words, taking my first steps, getting a certificate at school or later getting into university, graduating, getting jobs, getting published. I have no doubt that when my dad looks at me, he thinks I am beautiful.

You should never underestimate the importance of a father's words to his daughter. The words he utters as he brings up a girl can have the power to instil in her a sense of her own beauty, and build her up into the woman that she can become. Alternatively, his words can break her, so that she is left forever feeling inadequate, ugly. The role of a father in a woman's life is enormous. A caring, affirming, loving father just like our heavenly one can help to shape his daughter's amazing future, can help her to see herself as precious, unique. An uncaring, distant or abusive father can have a detrimental effect on his daughter's self-esteem.

> You should never underestimate the importance of a father's words to his daughter.

We hear that fathers should tell their daughters that they are beautiful because it will help raise their self-esteem. But we also hear that fathers should not tell their daughters they are beautiful too often for fear that they might start to find their identity only in their prettiness. What an important burden that our fathers carry on their shoulders.

Right now, my dad is the man in my life. I know, however, that he is biased. He thinks me and my sisters are clever and beautiful because he's programmed to think that way.

I think that God, like my earthly father, cares. While it may seem frivolous to worry about what I look like, he cares that there are times when it gets me down. He is my number one fan. He cheers me on and doesn't like it when I sit out the game because I'm so entangled in low self-esteem. There are bigger battles to fight. There are captives to be freed. There are widows and orphans to care for. There's justice to be seen. There is life to live in its fullness.

Validation From Men

When I asked my friends whether they felt beautiful and how they felt about their bodies, I was struck by the number of them who said they feel beautiful because of what their husbands or boyfriends tell them. They feel validated because someone tells them every day that they are beautiful.

One woman said: 'I have a lovely husband who takes the time every day to make sure I know I am beautiful both on the inside and out through complimenting me. There are of course days when I don't like what I see, but I have to remember that it's a temporary point of view and that my value doesn't solely come from what I look like – or at least it shouldn't.'

Another simply said: 'I feel beautiful when my husband compliments me.'

I love men. They are actually some of my favourite people. I enjoy male company at times more than I like hanging out with the girls. They are funny, easy to be with; they seem to have fewer hang-ups. As the oldest of three daughters, I have filled a place by my dad's side as the surrogate boy – his partner in watching football, his sidekick in carrying heavy objects down from the loft. My life has been marked by significant male friendships. I've gravitated towards great groups of guy friends and am comfortable being the only girl in a huddle of men. I like the attention that it brings me. I like the fact that I can feel protected, safe.

And that's what men are great at. When you're special to them, they can make you feel like the most beautiful girl in the world. When you're in a relationship with a good man, he can boost your self-esteem like no number of self-help books can. It's why so many women have based their feelings about their own beauty on what the men in their lives say about them. Thank God for men who boost self-esteem.

Thank God for men who boost self-esteem.

But when your self-validation is wrapped up in what he says about you rather than what He says about you, it can result in pain and feelings of inadequacy. The truth of this was made real to me as, alongside reading the stories of women who said they felt beautiful because their significant other told them they were, I read those of broken women whose feelings about their own beauty were tangled up with past attitudes, hurts and words spoken about them by boys and men – intentionally or unintentionally.

One of my friends told me: 'When I was at school, some boys used to call me Eurotunnel nose and it's affected the way I have seen my nose since. I have had prayer about it, but still don't really like it.' She is still carrying the hurt and pain from what was said about her by boys when she was a child. Words that tell us that we are un-beautiful can cut to the core of what it is to be valued. We feel ashamed, rejected and unloved.

Jennie Frost explains: 'Often people talk about bullying, abuse and other situations where they have been fed messages about themselves which are untrue. This can have a huge effect on body image. And sometimes when we are not happy with our lives, in whatever way that might be, our body image can take a hit as it is the physical reflection of the inner.'

I think about the times when I have felt most happy – they have often been times when I have felt good about the way I look, as well as about the great things happening in my life or the people that are making life great. But when I'm bored, unsatisfied, lonely, my mind often fixates on how I feel about my body. It's hard to know what comes first. Does a negative view of my body make me unhappy or am I unhappy because I think I'm un-pretty? It's impossible to know. But there are certainly enemies that exacerbate a negative sense of self. For example, 1 in 4 women will experience domestic violence in their lifetime, and, for many of these women, the abuse will also be verbal and psychological. Some men will choose to attack a woman's sense of beauty, to call her 'fat', 'ugly', 'repulsive' – because these words are among those that can hurt us the most.

It's a problem of perspective. We live in a broken world full of flawed, awful human beings – male and female – and the words we say to each other can cut so deeply. But it's the words of other people that seem so present. Sometimes God feels distant and we can't hear him because he seems so far away. All we hear is the fuzz of other people's words and criticisms. But we need to re-tune our dials to get a clear frequency and make an effort to hear the eternal truths that he whispers. His words are the truth: we are loved, we are precious, we are valuable and we are beautiful in his sight.

> His words are the truth: we are loved, we are precious, we are valuable and we are beautiful in his sight.

There's a line in the Bible that has always niggled at me. It's in the creation story, after the Fall when Eve is told that her desire will be for her husband and he will rule over her. What does that mean?

I've always read it to mean that there is something in women that craves the attention of men, a desire for them. And the fact that he rules over her represents an unfeeling, unloving man; maybe one who doesn't even notice her desire. Is that what God intended and does the curse of Eve apply to women today?

I'm glad to see that I'm not the only person who struggles to understand this passage. Some scholars have suggested it is probably the most difficult passage in the whole of Genesis and they have come up with different interpretations as to what it might mean. What I think it represents is the relationship between man and woman gone wrong. A woman craving after her husband, her eyes looking up at him looking down on her, is not how God intended it. This is a consequence of the Fall.

So does that mean that women today, the daughters of Eve, are under the same curse? If we still experience pain during childbirth – the other curse God talks about for women – will our desire still be for man and will he still rule over us? Maybe. Maybe that explains why so many of us crave affirmation from men. But we need to realize that that's not how it was intended. We live in the now-and-not-yet of the Kingdom of God. Christ came to redeem and renew all things, including our relationships, which means that in the Kingdom of God, which arrived when Jesus came but will be fulfilled when he comes again, we will seek affirmation from God and not from man.

How does all this help me now? It helps me to realize that an unhealthy craving for a man's attention isn't how it's supposed to be. And it frees me to recognize when the craving starts to rise, to take note and remember that his affirmation is temporary and unsatisfactory in the long run, while *His* affirmation is eternal and makes me feel whole.

Affirmation from the Ether

Today I changed my profile picture. And waited. The photograph had been taken on a night out with a group of friends. When I scrolled through the photos when I came home, I realized that most of them were not so good. A couple had caught me at the wrong moment, when my face was contorted – or in that not-so-pretty moment a split second before a blink or a yawn. A couple had me slouching so the wobbly bits were not as hidden as I would have liked. But this one photo; it was really good. The kind of photo where everything works together for good. I looked pretty. Everything poised. Great lighting, sparkly eyes, belly in, chin up. So, assigning the duff photos of me to the trash bin, I created a new album of our night out. I clicked 'make my profile photo' on *that* picture.

> I waited for someone to comment with a 'wow', 'gorgeous' or 'stunning'.

And I waited.

I waited for someone to 'like' it.

I waited for someone to comment with a 'wow', 'gorgeous' or 'stunning'.

I waited for one of my Facebook friends to tell me I was *beautiful*. But nothing.

Silence.

Maybe I was mistaken. Maybe the photo wasn't so great after all. Maybe no one was on Facebook at that particular moment. So maybe they would comment when they saw my photo on their news feed.

Still silence.

Maybe it hadn't uploaded properly. Should I upload it again? Had I messed up the privacy settings so no one could actually see the photo? Maybe there were too many things happening on Facebook. Eventually, they'd get round to mine.

Still. Nothing.

Maybe people don't like the photo. Maybe I have that body dysmorphia where I think I look good when no one else thinks so. Maybe I'm not so beautiful after all.

These are the types of crazy thoughts that go through my head when I put another piece of myself out there online; when I seek affirmation from the ether. For the most part, we blame the media, the fashion industry and the advertising industry for pedalling the beauty myth and for making women feel inadequate. But, if I'm really honest, in my everyday life, it's the online profiles of others – my friends – that make me feel most like I don't measure up. If I were to be totally honest, my Facebook profile is the main gauge by which I measure whether or not I am beautiful.

When I was a teenager and went to a party, I'd get dressed up, I'd put on some make-up, I'd have a good time with friends, I'd take photos. And at some point a few days or weeks later, I'd get the photos developed. Maybe I would like the photos. Maybe I wouldn't. But no one else had to see them. I was left to measure my own attractiveness. But Facebook changed all this. There are more than a billion Facebook users in the world today. That's a billion people logging on, sharing their lives and their likes with hundreds of 'friends'. Close friends, church friends, neighbours, acquaintances, colleagues, former friends, former partners, employers. Facebook is a gift for nosey people-lovers like me. I like its connectivity. I like that it feeds my constant craving for news. In September 2012, the social networking site's first ever TV advert told me that Facebook is a good thing, one of the best things. It told me that we need Facebook just like we need 'bridges' and 'chairs' and 'doorbells' and 'telephones'. Soothing my existential anxiety, it told me that I need Facebook so that I do not feel alone in the 'vast and dark' universe. Facebook is a good thing.

But we only have to look to the reason why Facebook was created to understand its more sinister roots and to realize the reasons why it has the ability to make us feel ugly, inadequate and anxious.

I'm one of those people whose weight has fluctuated dramatically over the years. And thanks to Facebook, you can quite easily track that fluctuation. Sometimes I consider de-tagging myself in the photos where I am at my heaviest, so that I can pretend they have not really happened. But then I choose to keep them there as a reminder and as a way for me to track when I'm creeping up towards that weight again.

The controversial Facebook timeline feature allows me to do that with ease. Thank you Mark Zuckerberg . . .

But this really isn't that good for my self-esteem, as a recent study found. According to a survey of around six hundred 16- to 40-year-old Facebook users undertaken by the Center for Eating Disorders at Sheppard Pratt, the social networking site does pretty well at making us feel bad about our bodies.

Around 75 per cent of the users said they were unhappy with their current weight. And half said seeing photos of themselves online definitely made them more aware of their weight. A third said they felt sad when they compared their own pictures with those of their friends.

And then there are those darned targeted ads. Facebook knows me. It knows I am a female in my late 20s. It knows that I am single. It knows that I go on the odd diet. It knows that – like most women my age – there are things I wish I could change about myself and this might manifest itself in my Google searches or the websites I look at.

I log onto my Facebook account a few times a day – maybe more than a few – and more often than not, there will be an advert about weight loss, or laser teeth whitening. There will also be adverts promising to find me the man of my dreams via some dating site or singles event. Darn you Facebook for playing on my insecurities!

All these little things are like whispers constantly suggesting to us that we need this or we need that, or that our lives would be better if only we had a certain something. They are suggestions that we are not beautiful as we are.

If you've seen the movie *The Social Network* you'll be familiar with the story of how Facebook began. It all started with Mark Zuckerberg, a student at Harvard who created Facemash – a website where the attractiveness of his fellow students could be rated by others. Facemash was a game that placed two students' faces side by side and asked the player to decide who was 'hot' and who was 'not'. When Facemash was created in 2003, Zuckerberg wrote on his blog, likening some women to 'farm animals'.

Farm animals?

I know women. And I know how damaging the effect would be of being compared to a farm animal. I know that would be an insult that would be hard to shrug off. It's hard to feel beautiful when you've been publicly humiliated. These were Harvard undergraduates, already battling with the pressures of competition and the inner questions *Am I beautiful? Am I clever? Am I of worth?* And they were being hit with a resounding 'No. You are not hot. You are *not.*'

These were the beginnings of a phenomenon that has swept the globe and that forms a major part of our daily lives. Every day, every status, every 'like', every comment, every friend request, every photo album, every tag, every check-in, every chat message screams of a deep-seated need to feel valued; to feel loved, to feel beautiful. It shouts 'Hey, look at me, aren't I great? Tell me I'm great. Tell me you want to be me. Tell me you wish you had the life I have.'

Last week, I decided to try again. I uploaded a new profile photo. And this one went down a treat. There were lots of comments telling me how great I looked. I got the 'wows', 'beauti-fuls' that I had hoped I would get by uploading it; but of course I feigned humility. 'You think I look beautiful? Hardly!' And I felt that familiar feeling

There will always be someone with more 'likes'.

– my ego being inflated; puffed up. A fleeting sense of feeling valued, loved, beautiful. A momentary sense that I was great, actually.

But when we get our affirmation from things of little value, such as Facebook profile photos, we are playing a dangerous game. Because there will always be someone with more 'likes'. We will constantly crave that affirmation and feel deflated when our egos are not soothed by people telling us how great we are, how gorgeous, how beautiful. When we seek value in such things, we will always be left feeling disappointed. Facebook is a reminder that our true worth can be found in one thing alone – our identity in Christ, and our worth as far as God is concerned.

Because what he says about us never changes. It never wavers. It doesn't think we're OK today and not so much tomorrow. It is a constant, never-ending 'like'.

No More Shame

I was the first girl in my class in primary school to get my period. I somehow seemed to skip the training bra phase and was the first to have to wear one of the real contraptions, which chafed and constricted while I was still very much trying to be a carefree girl. A girl developing a woman's body before I was ready. I don't remember being happy about it. At all. While some of my friends longed to become women, I felt an overwhelming sense of shame, as if my body were betraying me. I felt isolated and embarrassed and afraid of what was happening.

> I felt an overwhelming sense of shame, as if my body were betraying me.

There is a paradox that exists in how the world views the female body. In different contexts and communities around the world, a woman's body is considered to possess a certain inherent beauty. But while a woman is seen as beautiful, her body is also seen as something mysterious and something to be feared. Men are taught to be fearful of a woman's natural functions. We're all familiar with the somewhat damaging idea in popular psychology that women are hormonal, irrational, over-sensitive and crazy and so should be handled with care by the men in their lives. And these men are also taught to excuse themselves from any talk of menstruation, breastfeeding, childbirth and the menopause. These things are *other*, to be discussed only within the otherworldly secret arena known as 'girl-talk'.

Old Testament purity laws outline the regulations about female impurity during menstruation. We read that a woman is impure for the seven days from when her period starts and that anyone who touches a menstruating woman is rendered unclean. There are similar laws concerning how women should be kept separate during their menstrual flow in non-Judaeo-Christian societies around the world. Tomi-Ann Roberts, a psychologist at Colorado College in Colorado Springs, undertook a study which found that, although religious communities with strict regulations about menstruation made women feel more ashamed, they increased female bonding in those communities.[29] While secular Western societies appear not to be as uptight when it comes to women's periods, there is still an unwritten sense of secrecy and shame surrounding them. She added that with this cloud of otherworldliness, mystery and shame surrounding such female physical functions as menstruation comes a negative view of a woman's body.

Just think of all the things that a woman's body does: it bleeds and it lactates. Although it has to do these things to create new life, the manner in which it does this isn't very beautiful. At least that's what the world would have us believe. No wonder girls feel so ashamed of their bodies. Periods are not to be mentioned in polite society, and you're expected to do everything not to show that you have them. Breastfeeding is also taboo and will have people squirming in their seats if you talk about it.

The concept of the flawed female body, complete with its alien and mysterious functions, is also deeply rooted in the history of the church. In the early church, women were thought incapable of joining the priesthood 'by virtue of the fact that their rational souls were housed in female bodies rather than male ones, and they were therefore incapable of symbolizing Christ as the embodiment of perfect humanity'.[30] Maybe we have been conditioned to believe that because the female body is imperfect, it's something to be criticized, mocked and derided because it is flawed. Perhaps that is what's behind the feeling that arises when I step on the scales or see myself in an unflattering position in the changing room of a department store; that sense that rises up in me when I feel an overwhelming pang of jealousy towards someone more beautiful; and the embarrassment I feel about my body's femaleness. All such feelings boil down to one thing: shame.

Shame researcher Brené Brown writes: 'Shame is the intensely painful feeling or experience of believing that we are flawed and therefore unworthy of love and belonging.'[31] We should not underestimate the power of feeling shame when it comes to understanding our body image, shattered self-image and low self-esteem. The sense that we are unclean, imperfect, flawed, unattractive, unloveable and un-beautiful lingers at the back of our minds whether we are aware of it or not. Brown carried out interviews with 200 very different women and found that all of their shame experiences fitted into 10 categories: identity, sexuality, family, motherhood, appearance, parenting, health, ageing, the ability to stand up and speak out for herself and religion. She found that around 90 per cent of the participants had experienced shame about their bodies – body shame made an appearance in all of the categories. 'What we think, hate, loathe and wonder about the acceptability of our bodies reaches much further and impacts far more than our appearance. The long reach of body shame can impact who and how we love, work, parent, communicate and build relationships.'[32]

Shame is powerful. In every definition, it is described as painful, something that hurts. It is a feeling and therefore something that we have a sensation of in our physical bodies. Shame therefore betrays us

> All such feelings boil down to one thing: shame.

by manifesting itself in our physical behaviour. Rodin's life-size sculpture of Eve after the Fall is a haunting illustration of shame. In 1928, poet Rainer Marie Rilke described the sculpture: 'From a distance she seems to be enfolded in her arms, with hands turned to the outside as if to push away everything, even her own changing body.'

Shame paralyses us. It stops us in our tracks. Shame makes us hide away in self-preservation. Shame makes us cover ourselves up, like Adam and Eve did, shielding ourselves from what we're sure is coming our way – the exposure and the punishment that we are certain we deserve for our imperfection in the presence of perfection.

> Shame paralyses us. It stops us in our tracks.

When my friend Renee, who runs the Devotional Diva blog, was growing up, she had such severe eczema it took the skin off her feet, hands and face. She had to take Prednisone to control the condition, which caused her to pile on more than 100 pounds in just 10 months. She was ashamed of the way she looked. 'I felt that no one would love me, that I was not beautiful,' she says. 'My body made me feel ugly.' But God drew her close to him and in relationship with him she found truth. She found the truth that through his wounds she was healed. That she was free from shame. That she was beautiful. 'Because of what I've been through with my body, I no longer see beauty in the way the world sees it. I love my body not because it's perfect, but because of its battle scars. And that is beautiful.'

Go in Peace

Twelve years. That's how long the woman in the Mark 5 account had been suffering with her female-only ailment. The 'issue' of her bleeding isolated her and filled her with shame. She had tried everything, spending a lot of money, to make her body acceptable, good again. There was one thing, one person, she hadn't tried yet. So, fighting her way through the crowds as he was walking past, she desperately reached out to touch the hem of his coat. And with this encounter – even with his cloak – her bleeding immediately stopped. Though her physical body was healed, she was not yet free. Jesus still had a work to do in her. He wanted to see her, to speak to her, to speak words of freedom over her. Because he knew that it was only through really seeing him face to face that she would be free indeed. 'Go in peace and be freed from your suffering,' he said to her. She was freed physically, she was made whole and then she went – in peace. Shalom. Whole.

Our flawed body image, our craving for beauty – and the sense of shame that accompanies these – are only in part about our physical bodies. Once again beauty is only part of the story. Because shame is part of the human condition, something we all experience. It is that feeling that we are not good enough, that we are somehow faulty, bad, that we are unworthy and incapable of being loved, that we are condemned.

But this is where grace comes in: 'Therefore, there is now no condemnation for those who are in Christ Jesus' (Rom. 8:1). This perfect grace redeems us from that overpowering sense of shame about our bodies and shame about our flawed humanity so that we are freed from that familiar feeling of constant condemnation. Because the truth is that we *are* imperfect. Our sinful nature is not beautiful. As Philip Yancey writes: 'Imperfection is the prerequisite for grace. Light only gets in through the cracks.'[33] And this light will get in. It really wants to get into those cracks. But we have to let it. We have to allow God to make our imperfections perfect. Though we don't feel beautiful in ourselves or in our bodies, we have to take a deep breath, let the cracks show and let him make them beautiful.

In this chapter we have explored some of the enemies that get in the way of us feeling beautiful: shame, low self-esteem and seeking affirmation from things and people other than God, comparing ourselves to others and being jealous of them. In 1 Peter 5:8 we read: 'Be alert and of sober mind. Your enemy the devil prowls around like a roaring lion looking for someone to devour.' Reading this is a reminder that we need to watch out for these enemies, be conscious of the times when we are being sucked in and wary that there is someone actively seeking to steal our joy and render us ineffective for the Kingdom.

Thank God that we are not powerless against these enemies and that we can fight back against them, refusing to be drawn in.

Prayer

Dear Father Lord,

Thank you for 'liking' me – no matter what I look like. I choose to seek affirmation only in you. Lord, please help me to find it. May I be satisfied only in your love for me. May I forever look for your face in all things. Thank you that you delight over me; that your plans for me are for good and not to harm me. Lord, would you father me, would you come alongside me and show me what it is to be valued, to be affirmed. I pray for the men in my life. May their words speak affirmation and goodness to me. But, ultimately, help me to see my sense of worth is only found in you – not in others, not in my online persona, not in comments about how I look. Thank you for your love for me. It is enough. Thank you that because it is enough, no longer can these compliments or achievements – or a lack of them – make me any more or less loved. Protect me from the enemies of low self-esteem, shame, comparison and jealousy. I have no need of them. Help me to remember this. And help me to help others find the amazing truth that they are valued, forever validated, by you – the lover of our souls.

Amen

Questions to Ponder

- Renee Fisher talks about the physical battle scars signifying what she has been through. What stories do your own battle scars tell about your life?
- In *The Freedom of Self-Forgetfulness* Tim Keller says that someone who repeatedly says that they are a nobody is really a self-obsessed person. Do you agree that self-esteem is actually self-centeredness?
- Name your enemy: which of the things we have discussed in this chapter do you most struggle with? Find a Bible verse to combat that and stick it on your mirror for a month, meditating on it every day.
- Try to write a realistic picture of yourself and ask a close friend for their input/comments afterwards. How does it make you feel to read it through?
- What are you most ashamed of? Write it down on a piece of paper. Ponder Romans 8:1. Rip up the piece of paper. How do you feel?

Beauty Challenge

The next time you sense that you are jealous of someone, give them a compliment instead of letting the green-eyed monster fester inside you.

6.

Ages and Stages of Beauty

Am I Beautiful? I have been beautiful since I was a little girl, I am beautiful now and I will still be beautiful as I grow older. The world tells me that I should fear the future and do everything I can to preserve the beauty of youth. It tells me that the stages of life that I go through make me less beautiful and not more. But God tells me that everything is beautiful in its time.

'The beauty of a woman is not in a facial mode, but the true beauty in a woman is reflected in her soul. It is the caring that she lovingly gives, the passion that she shows. The beauty of a woman with passing years only grows.' (Audrey Hepburn)

'We delight in the beauty of the butterfly, but rarely admit the changes it has gone through to achieve that beauty.' (Maya Angelou)

'Gray hair is a crown of glory; it is gained in a righteous life.' (Proverbs 16:31, NRSV)

The Big 3-0

I am sitting in my flat amid the rubble of my 29th birthday party. I had a blast, a perfect night; partying the night away with my favourite people. I don't understand people who choose not to celebrate their birthdays. I've always loved mine. It's an annual excuse to get friends from my different walks of life together with the attention all on me. What's not to love? But there was an unfamiliar feeling this time as I approached my birthday this year, 29 seemingly hurtling towards me much faster than previous birthdays have. I didn't feel I was ready for this, the final year of my 20s. How had this happened? It felt like only yesterday when I graduated from university, bright-eyed and optimistic about the future. I don't feel very different from the 10-year-old girl who made friendship bracelets and passed notes in class. I remember being so desperate to turn 10 (double digits), to turn 13 (become a teenager), to turn 16 (that sweet age), to turn 17 (get a drivers' licence), to turn 18 (an adult), to turn 21 (a real adult), to turn 25 (a real, proper adult). With the promise of each of these ages came the hope that I would somehow become a little bit more sorted. But I still feel lost. So how can it be that I am just a year away from the big 3-0?

When shopping for the outfit I wore to my party, I'm ashamed to admit that I also bought a super-tummy-sucking-in-all-in-one-body-controlling-number. The scene in my bedroom before my party as I squeezed into this miracle worker was something to behold; hopping around like a madwoman as I determinedly tried to prize the underwear into place. The rather unladylike fastening of the popper buttons strategically placed in the nether regions to ensure I would be able to go to the loo. But as I stood unable to breathe, having successfully squeezed myself in, I knew there would be no such visits to the loo. The constricting body suit would make it difficult to make any movements at all. It was worth it, though, as I effortlessly slipped into the lacy black dress, lumps and bumps smoothed over underneath. I guess this is the kind of thing a lady has to do when she approaches her 30s!

I'm scared of 30. I'm scared because I live in a society in which the archetype of a beautiful woman is one in her 20s. And I never quite felt like I was that archetype anyway. I'm scared of 30 because I live in a world that makes such a big thing of leaving your 20s, as if you are saying goodbye to the best years of your life, your prettiest days now being behind you. I'm scared that the skin on my face will crack and sag, that it will wrinkle. I'm scared that my hair will start to go grey, that my body will become frail, that I won't be able to do all the things I used to be able to.

Some of my friends have resorted to taking pre-emptive action to combat the ageing process. One recently told me that I should really start thinking about having a 'skin regime', complete with night creams and the like. Night cream? That's the kind of thing my grandma owns. But it's got me worried. Maybe I should see what's available. Because maybe I am worth it. But a quick search and the number of products on offer is overwhelming. Re-plumping night cream, anti-wrinkle serum with hyaluronic acid. There are eyelid lift strips, titanium micro-needles, derma skin rollers, collagen crystal face masks – all written in code so that you don't really know what you're putting on your face but feel you ought to anyway.

> Why do so many women feel the need to hide the ageing process rather than celebrate it?

Because in a world where beauty is youth, and that youth is placed on a pedestal, nobody wants to grow old. Or at least nobody wants to look like they are growing old. We are on a quest to remain forever young, and this search for the elixir of youth has caused the anti-aging industry to swell rapidly. By 2015, the market for anti-ageing products for appearance enhancement is set to be worth $5 billion – and that's in just one country.[34] That makes me sick, considering the UN estimates it would take just $30 billion a year to end global hunger.

Why do so many women feel the need to hide the ageing process rather than celebrate it? I felt there was no better person to explore this question with than the fabulous author and theologian Michele Guinness.

'Women need to be looked at,' she tells me. We are sitting in her home, curled up in the living room on a cold winter's night. I'm struck by just how tiny and stunning this woman is. It's hard to believe she is a grandmother. Her bright eyes dance as she regales me with tales from her past. 'In the year I was 25, I got four proposals,' she tells me. She had gone from being described as a 'plain' child to being a hot young thing in her 20s. 'Being seen as attractive made a huge difference to my life. I began to see myself differently and I began to be aware of that. I was starting to be approached by men for the first time. It made me feel very confident. I was flamboyant and wore bright colours and I have quite a noticeable face because I'm Jewish and there weren't many Jewish faces around when I was young. So men would look at me.'

But as she grew older she started to realize things were changing. 'Suddenly you notice that, as the years go by, the age of the men looking at you increases. Men in their 20s don't look at me now. It's men in their 60s and 70s! And suddenly it stops altogether. And that can be a real slap in the face if it's something you're used to. It can be very, very hard. As you get older, you become invisible as a woman. You are not you anymore. It's a huge issue. We do need to be looked at. We do need to have somebody notice us in whatever way that is. We need to be taken seriously as individuals.'

I think this is what scares me most about the thought of growing old. Not being seen. Being ignored and seen as irrelevant, outdated and past it. I'm angry that I live in a world that causes me to fear the future rather than welcome it with open arms.

I'm so thankful that I can see a beautiful future ahead of me just by looking at two women that have paved the way before me: my mum and my grandma. Over the years I've become increasingly fascinated with how our very different lives are intertwined, how we are similar women spread across the ages. My grandma, Patience Ene, lives in Enugu in Nigeria. She is 79 and has 7 children, 20 grandchildren and 4 great-grandchildren, living all over the world. My grandma and grandfather were very much a part of the African elite in the 1950s and 1960s, sipping cocktails, having tea parties, playing golf with 'the set' and jetting off to the capital for swanky dinner parties. I love looking at old black and white photographs of them back in those days, my grandmother stunningly beautiful and my grandfather tall, handsome and dashing.

> I'm angry that I live in a world that causes me to fear the future rather than welcome it with open arms.

I try to get some beauty tips from grandma over the phone. Hers seem pretty simple to me at first: 'Clean your face and wear nice clothes.' But she adds: 'There's nobody that looks beautiful without effort.' She is almost exactly 50 years older than I am. As she approaches 80, she seems to have settled on her keys to being beautiful. 'I aim to look natural even when I'm wearing make-up. However you are, you can be attractive. I don't want to look young. I'm old. Just enhance what God gave you and then be happy. Look nice for yourself. Attracting men is not the ultimate aim – none of them are looking at me anyway.'

My grandfather died when granny was 48, a few years before I was born. I try to imagine what that must have been like for her. She tells me that at the time it felt like her world had ended. But it shaped her into the feisty, passionately praying great-grandmother that she is today.

My mother Stella, her eldest child, was very much a part of that strengthening process. They helped each other through the pain of losing my grandfather. Granny remembers the day my mum was born – a 'beautiful baby with tight curly black hair and very long fingers'. 'It was like a miracle,' she tells me. 'I was very proud.' That beautiful baby girl went on to have three beautiful baby girls of her own – I was one of them. She also became the first black female principal of a further education college in the UK and was honoured with a CBE by Her Majesty the Queen herself a few years ago.

But it's her own mother who instilled in her a sense that she was beautiful and smart and capable of doing anything. 'My mother taught me to walk tall,' she says to me. 'I used to tower above everybody else when I was young, and so developed a bit of a stoop due to trying to make myself look smaller. But your grandma told me I should walk tall and be proud of who I am. I've tried to pass this on to my own daughters. I've tried to show them they can walk tall too and be anything and everything they want to be.'

Here is where my mother's story echoes mine. My struggle to make myself smaller, the anxiety caused by standing out from the crowd and being different. But my mother, too, taught me to be proud of who I am. To walk tall. Never to slouch.

Celebrating Motherhood

Mothers and grandmothers are to be celebrated. In my humble opinion the body of the female of the species is more beautiful than the male's because it has the ability to incubate, bring forth and nurture new life. Childbirth is a wonderful demonstration of the beauty of a woman's body. But such is the nature of our beauty-distorting society that this most wondrous of occasions is accompanied by negativity about how the woman's body will be ruined in the process. Celebrity magazines and social media have added to the pressure on new mothers.

And some are succumbing to that pressure more than others. I was stunned when a friend drew my attention to a blog post by a woman called Kate Williams who revealed that when she found out that she was expecting, her mind immediately turned to thoughts of her appearance. 'When I found out that my due date was May 1st,' she wrote, 'my first thoughts weren't of baby blankets and onesies. All I could think about was, how am I going to avoid looking like a wet dish towel in one of those post-delivery photos?'[35] She then proceeds to take us through the lengths she went to in order to prepare for that photo in the post entitled 'How to Look Great During Childbirth.'

Postpartum photographs are becoming increasingly popular, thanks to the rise of social media. I'm always amazed at friends of mine who post their brand new mummy photos on Facebook just minutes after pushing out their babies, looking stunning. The pre-occupation with how mums look is accompanied by an ever-increasing pressure to look great before, during and after giving birth.

For example, there are few things as revered in celebrity gossip columns as a hot post-baby body. It seems women in the public eye compete to see who can lose their postpartum weight the fastest. We look on in awe at the new mums posing in bikinis seemingly just days after they were in the delivery room. We're wowed by these 'mom-shells' because their svelte bodies seem to contravene the laws of nature. They are amazing. New mums shouldn't look so 'good'. But the proliferation of these stories makes the rapid return to pre-baby bodies seem like the norm, isolating those women who do not 'get their body back' fast enough – if at all – and making them seem like failures.

> Everyday women, including women in the church, can feel a sense of peer pressure from the example of these celebrity mums.

Actress Hilary Duff took – shock horror – eight months to get back into her 26-inch skinny jeans. And because she 'took her time' doing it, with the help of a daily personal trainer and gruelling exercise regime, the celebrity magazines seemed to celebrate her finally reaching her goal weight. Go Hilary!

The all-pervasive nature of modern media means that everyday women, including women in the church, can feel a sense of peer pressure from the example of these celebrity mums.

I am not a mother. I've never given birth, nor have I ever been pregnant. But several of my friends have. And I have realized that I, too, am guilty of giving women the once-over when I see them for the first time after they've had their baby. I expect them not to look great, to look less than their former selves. And those who do look great are met with surprised and almost bewildered compliments from me about how good they look – you know – considering . . .

As far as society's concerned, women give up their bodies when they have children. And of course it's a price worth paying. But these women are the same ones who, before they became mummies, longed to feel valued, of worth, they were those who craved beauty. Motherhood doesn't change that at all. Our inner longings remain the same. But motherhood does change your body. In ways that I am yet to understand. Around half of the women I spoke to said they felt worse about their bodies after they had children.

I may not be a mother, but I am an extremely broody single woman. I love babies and one day hope to have my own brood. But the second most scary prospect of becoming a mother – after the horrific-sounding giving birth part – is that my body, with which I already struggle, could become even 'worse'. Despite the scariness of the prospect, I know that it will all be worth it to become someone's mummy.

I asked friends of mine who are already mummies to tell me how they felt about their bodies, whether they felt pressure either from our celebrity culture or their own friends. One friend tells me that she was pretty confident before she had her first child. 'Two babies later and I have zero confidence in how I look,' she says. 'It's a pretty weird thing to get my head around as I've never really experienced such low self-esteem.' She says it's not the celebrities that get her down as they have access to personal trainers, nutritionists and cleaners. They are getting help in all areas of their life. Instead, it's other mums that cause her to feel bad about her own body. 'It's the comparison to mummy friends that gets to me – wondering how people managed to get such tiny little waists so short a time after having a baby. In spite of this, I'm proud of what my body has achieved and feel stronger and more capable than ever, even if I think the current body is not as beautiful.'

It's strange for me to get a taster of the internal monologues that are going on inside my friends' heads. I look at them and think they have got it all, or at least all the things I want: the husband and the cute children. But really they have the same insecurities as me when it comes to their bodies, pressure and comparison once again rearing their ugly heads. The need to feel beautiful does not stop once you start a family.

Another friend seems to have it in perspective. After putting on two stone with each of her pregnancies and taking a couple of years each time to return to her pre-pregnancy weight, she's let go of feeling jealous about other mums who regain their figures very soon after. 'All our bodies are different,' she says. 'I'm a big-boned woman. I am never going to be a size six, so why worry about it?'

> Motherhood means your life is totally changed forever. Your body is no longer your own.

Talking to these women makes me understand that becoming a mum is far more than having a cute baby to cuddle and dress up, which is what I think about on my broody days. Motherhood means your life is totally changed forever. Your body is no longer your own. Ruth used to run marathons before she got pregnant. Although she lost her baby weight within a month, the abs she had sculpted through her strenuous exercise regime were 'shot to pieces', she tells me. Her new lifestyle as a mother has further changed her body. 'I eat more as I'm at home and less active than I was at work, plus my baby's needs come first so if there's only enough time for one of us to have breakfast, she has hers and I grab two bourbon creams on my way out the door – same goes for getting make-up and hair done too.' Despite the lack of exercise and lack of abs, Ruth is pretty amazed by her body. 'I feel a lot more relaxed now because I have a new respect for it,' she says. 'It grew a baby, pushed one out drug-free and then fed her despite great difficulties – the least I can do is give it some carbs and a chocolatey treat every once in a while.'

The Next Generation

If I ever have daughters, I want them to know that they are beautiful. I don't want them to even give it a second thought. I don't want them to face the anguish and pain that so many women of my generation and previous generations have faced, all because of a sense of feeling un-beautiful. I don't want it to hold them back from being the women they could be, from changing the world. As I battle with my own body image issues, I read stories of young girls who despise their bodies, who are desperate to look like glamour models or television stars or who feel that they should at least want to look that way. And my heart aches for them.

I think of the beautiful girls in the youth group at my church or my young girl cousins and I just know that they are going through the same battles as we have gone through and we continue going through. And I think that at some point this has got to stop. It *has* to stop. But it will take some radical changes to ensure that our daughters and their daughters don't have to go through this.

The radical step starts with believing that we are beautiful and modelling that belief in our own beauty. It will mean no longer accepting thinking we are un-beautiful as the norm. It means showing that we are happy with ourselves, thanks very much. And it also means challenging those words and images that might make these younger women feel inadequate, unworthy and unloved.

Amanda King is modelling that radical belief about her own beauty as an example to her daughters. A mum-of-two from Pittsburgh who blogs regularly, she says: 'I am slow and I am tired. I am round and sagging. I am harried. I am sexless. I am getting older. I am beautiful. How can this be? How can any of this be true? I don't want my girls to be children who are perfect and then, when they start to feel like women, they remember how I thought of myself as ugly and so they will be ugly too. They will get older and their breasts will lose their shape and they will hate their bodies, because that's what women do. That's what mommy did. I want them to become women who remember me modelling impossible beauty. Modelling beauty in the face of a mean world, a scary world, a world where we don't know what to make of ourselves. "Look at me, girls!" I say to them. "Look at how beautiful I am. I feel really beautiful, today."'[36]

> A mother has the power to shape her daughter's life.

This feels radical. Mums don't normally go around saying how beautiful they are. Such a scene seems unfamiliar somehow, because mothers are women and are therefore supposed to experience a sense of dissatisfaction with their own beauty. But what if we only think that because our mothers did? And what if they did because their own mothers did before them? Generations and generations of women perpetuating the lie that body hatred is part of what it is to be a woman. What if we could break that chain? Knowing how a mother has the power to shape her daughter's life and in turn those of the generations that come after her, it starts with us.

I want my gorgeous baby goddaughter Skye never to feel that she has to hate her body because she thinks that's what women are supposed to do. I want my beautiful and feisty goddaughter Osinachukwu to be forever confident in who she is. So I vow never to complain about the way I look in front of them. I vow never to focus solely on how cute and pretty they are, without also telling them that they are good, kind, precious and valuable. I feel a weight of responsibility for their future, because I know the importance of mothers and older female women in shaping girls' lives.

My friend Jo Saxton knows just how important an issue this is. She is a director at 3DM, which trains churches and Christian leaders, She is also the mother of two beautiful daughters and the author of *High Heels and Holiness* and *Influential*. I really wanted to find out from her how she manages to raise daughters in a world that tells them that they are judged by what they look like and not by what lies within. 'I guess I tackle this with broad brush strokes – there are a number of messages I want my daughters to grow up with. I want them to value health and wholeness, but to value wisdom, strength, confidence, boldness, intelligence, social skills, creative expression, their voice – above what someone may look like. Both parents and community play a role and we're committed to broadening the definition of beauty way beyond a clothes size/airbrushed image/skin tone. So we include all shapes and sizes, all ages and abilities, and we include character as well as physical traits. To me, wanting my daughters to just feel beautiful is too low a bar – they are stunning, but there's so much more to them than that.'

She tells me that she is pretty frustrated with the view in both society and the church that beauty is a women's *raison d'être*. 'Even we Christians get swept up and bound up by it. It's a lie, and distracts us from our God-given call as his representatives on earth.'

I'm surprised but heartened that she still thinks that it's vitally important for her daughters to feel that they are stunningly beautiful, without making it the most important thing in their young lives. She still tells them every day that they are beautiful, that she loves their hair, their style, their faces. But she also tells them 'that their little bodies are great and can do so much'. She's struck a balance that many people would find hard to do.

'I encourage and acknowledge the wonder of every stage of their physical development. I'll probably be the mama who takes my kids out for a fancy meal and shopping spree when puberty hits with a vengeance, because I want them to feel that their bodies are worth acknowledging and respecting. But I'm mindful that they hear other things too. I affirm when they are kind, when they are courageous, when they do well academically, when they share.'

Jo's own experience growing up makes her even more determined not to let her daughters go through the same feelings of un-prettiness. She is trying her best to break the cycle. 'When I look back, the media images and the playground were the most dominant voices,' she says. 'I was too dark, there was never anyone like me on the cover of a magazine. In school lighter-skinned girls were deemed attractive. Add to this that I was not wearing the most fashionable labels. I was never really viewed as pretty. It was a constant battle that took years to overcome. So while I'm in cute kid utopia right now, I'm aware other struggles will come. They will have different battles to me. My kids are bi-racial in the age of Obama – caramel is in. They may not feel quite the pressures I felt; but there will be other ones. Right now my commitment is to lay the strongest possible foundations, and skill them with all the tools they will need so that when the battle comes – we are ready and equipped. The rest we'll learn when we get there.

'And I think having two watchful daughters and co-pastoring a church with my husband makes me mindful of how I treat my body. But again, not just my body – myself. My mind, my health, my energy. I'm the example of womanhood that they see most closely in their growing up. And I'm very human with various failures – but that awareness does make me mindful of how I eat, dress and look after myself because since I am discipling them in these things, I need to have a life worth imitating! But again I want them to see most of all how a woman walks with God in every part of life.'

I want to live my life as if my goddaughters and my future daughters are watching. I want to be an example to them and be that woman who walks with God through every bit of life, including the beauty bit. I don't want them to go through the pain, insecurity, low self-esteem, shame, jealousy, comparison and inadequacy that I have experienced when I've looked in the mirror and looked at others around me and tried to measure up to society's arbitrary standard of beautiful. This book has been a process of wrestling with all of these things. I've laid bare some of the pains that I've kept hidden all of my life, and brought to the surface some of the things that have made me cry when I've been alone. I've done it all in the hope that I will find freedom, by taking the time to listen to eternal truths about who I am in Christ. Because I hope that the future will be better for women's sense of identity.

> I want to live my life as if my goddaughters and my future daughters are watching.

But why wait till then? All the things that I want for the women of the future, I also want for women of today. For you. My story is just one story. My struggle is just one struggle. There's nothing remarkable about it. In fact, part of the process for me has been realizing that my story is normal. So many of us are living this. Each of us has our own stories and our own struggles. But I'm hoping each of us can take steps towards being free from them, so they no longer become the norm in our lives and do not continue to be the norm in the lives of tomorrow's women.

I am beautiful.

And so are you.

Beautiful in Its Time

All throughout the book of Ecclesiastes, the writer – thought to be King Solomon – grapples with the futility of life. What's the point of it all? Seasons come, seasons go. It's all vanity, he cries. But then we come to 3:11 where he states: 'He has made everything beautiful in its time.' God has made everything full of beauty – all the things he has created display that beauty. And they are beautiful in whichever time is their time to be beautiful.

In the verses before this, he writes that there is a time for everything. A time to be born, a time to die; a time to plant and a time to uproot; a time to weep and a time to laugh; a time to mourn and a time to dance; a time to love and a time to hate; a time for war and a time for peace.

What can that tell me about my beauty journey? There is a time to be a girl, giggling and dressing up like a princess. There is a time to be a teenager, awkward about my changing body. There is a time for my 20s, enjoying my youth and looking forward to the future. There is a time for my 30s, my 40s, my 50s, my 60s, my 70s, my 80s and 90s. Each of these ages is in its own time and beauty develops rather than fades in each. Each has a different kind of beauty. But each is beautiful in its time, because our beauty is an everlasting beauty that comes only from being created by a beautiful God.

> Loving my body certainly has not come easily to me.

A Love Letter to My Body

While I know in my heart that I am beautiful because God made me, loving my body certainly has not come easily to me. You could say our love affair has been a tumultuous one.

Sure, we've had some fleeting dalliances – the odd glance in the mirror where I've caught sight of it and approved.

But on the whole, arriving at a place where I can say that I truly love my body has been a journey I've been travelling on most of my life.

When you start writing about beauty and body image, as I have done, and you start telling others to look at the inside and stop obsessing with the mirror, eventually there will come a time when you're forced to look at your own reflection, and honestly love what you see staring back at you.

The time is now for me and my body.

But let's get one thing clear: I can't do that fake flaunt-it-style sassy, body-confidence.

The kind that struts its stuff for the outside world, but hides those feelings of shame, guilt and inadequacy that are the reality for so many women when it comes to their relationships with their bodies.

My body and I don't do public displays of affection for other people's benefit. Ours is growing into a secure, steadfast kind of love.

Because when I say 'I love my body', I have to mean it.

Deeply.

Completely.

Unconditionally.

Wholly. Inside and out.

When I say 'I love my body', that love has to come from a place of authenticity, of deep understanding, of respect and acceptance.

It's a forever love, not a flirty crush. It doesn't wane as I grow older, as my body changes as my years increase.

When it comes to my relationship with my body, you could say that I have been that abusive partner that nobody would want to be in a relationship with.

I have put it down. I've beaten it up, trapped it, constrained it, hidden it. I've compared it to other, 'better' bodies. I have hated it.

I've ignored its appeals for affirmation.

Do you love me?

Yes, once you've lost another 10 pounds.

Do you love me?

Yes, as long as you're at the gym three times a week.

Do you love me?

You know I do, but just as long as you're dressed up in your most flattering clothes.

With each answer, I have denied my body the love and affirmation that it needs, and the praise that it deserves.

But right now, I'm standing at the altar, vowing to love my body, my constant friend and faithful partner. In sickness and in health, in good times and in bad, in joy as well as in sorrow. Forsaking all other body shapes, I promise to love my body unconditionally – through the weight gain and the weight loss, through the good hair days and the hat days, the wrinkles and the laughter lines, and maybe through childbirth someday.

I promise to cherish and protect my body through it all.

And I promise to love it. Not in a shout-it-from-the-rooftops kind of way. Not in a Tom-Cruise-jumping-up-and-down-on-Oprah's-sofa way.

But I will love it all the same. Quietly, confidently, deeply, fully; knowing that I am beautiful.

Because my body is created by God.

It is an outworking of his creativity and his beauty; it is a reflection of his image. This body – my body – is fearfully and wonderfully made. And he has called it 'good'.[37]

Prayer

Dear Lord,
Thank you that you have made me . . . me. I thank you that nothing can detract from me reflecting your beauty – not age, nor circumstance. I thank you for this beautiful body. I pray that your Holy Spirit will help me to love it now, forever, always.
Amen.

Questions to Ponder

- What was your response to Jo Saxton's ideas about raising daughters?
- At what age have you been the happiest with your body?
- How do you feel about getting older?
- Are you beautiful?
- Is there a younger woman in your church you can become a beauty mentor to? She can be your daughter, a niece, a goddaughter or a young girl you know well. Make time to tell her that she is beautiful, listen to any concerns she has about her body and encourage her in developing stunning inner beauty.
- How do you feel about your body, compared with five years ago, a decade ago, twenty years ago and how do you want to feel about it in twenty years' time?

Beauty Challenge

Having read my love letter to my body, it's now your turn. Write down the things you love about your body, remembering the journey that you've been on and looking forward to all that is to come.

Afterword:

Something Beautiful for God

Am I beautiful? When we feel secure, whole, valued and beautiful in our creator God, we no longer need to ask this question. And when we are free from seeking affirmation, feeling insecure about our bodies and craving beauty, we are free to be the culture-making, injustice-fighting, Christ-reflecting women we were created to be. That has to be our story.

'But saints and angels behold that glory of God which consists in the beauty of His holiness; and it is this sight only that will melt and humble the hearts of men, wean them from the world, draw them to God, and effectually change them.' (Jonathan Edwards, *Religious Affections*)

'No woman has ever changed the world by complaining about the size of her thighs.' (Sarah Silverman, Twitter 2012)

Changing the World

Being voted 'the pupil most likely to change the world' as I left school, aged 18, remains the proudest moment of my life so far. I didn't win 'most eligible female', nor was I considered the most likely to become a TV presenter. But my fellow class-mates thought that if anyone was going to change the world, I was. And I was truly honoured. Because, even though in my childhood I had longed to be pretty, to have long hair, to be slimmer and shorter, for the boys to ask me out; deep down, I really just wanted to make a difference. I wanted to make things better wherever I could. The craving to be beautiful was a story in my life, but it wasn't *the story*. The story is far bigger than that. The itch to make the world a better place has been with me for as long as I can remember. That's why I decided at the age of 13 that I wanted to be a journalist. Because journalism to me was about uncovering injustice, being a voice to the voiceless and holding authorities to account. I may not have seen what I wanted to when I looked in the mirror at myself, but I wanted to take that same mirror and hold it up to a society that I knew was broken and un-beautiful. I wanted to show up all the wrong things that were taking place, to shine a light on the dark and hidden places.

> The itch to make the world a better place has been with me for as long as I can remember.

We mock the contestants in beauty pageants for their clichéd wishes for 'world peace'. We look at them, hair coiffed to perfection, princess dresses flowing, their make-up pristine, and we think that they cannot really be serious about wanting to make the world a better place because if they were they wouldn't be so preoccupied with how they look. Beauty queens get a hard time, but, for some of them, beauty is only part of their story. In 2002, the Miss World contest was due to take place in Abuja, Nigeria – where I'm from. This was the first time an African nation had hosted the famous competition. But this, the 52nd pageant, was eventually moved to London because a number of the contestants had threatened to boycott it because of the case of Amina Lawal. Amina was a Nigerian woman from Kaduna in the predominantly Muslim north of the country who was due to be stoned to death for adultery for having a child outside marriage. A number of the contestants felt they could not take part in a beauty contest in a country where this was taking place, and pledged solidarity with Amina.

> 'When a woman faces the most agonizing death, there are more important things in life than winning a crown for being beautiful.'

Miss France, Sylvie Teller, said: 'When a woman faces the most agonizing death, there are more important things in life than winning a crown for being beautiful.' The truth is, there are always far more important things than being beautiful – things that need your attention in your street, your community, your country, your world. According to the UN, there are 900 million women and girls facing extreme poverty. Women own just 1 per cent of the world's wealth, we earn just 10 per cent of the world's income and half a billion of us can't read or write. But as Marianne Williamson, 'spiritual activist', author and founder of The Peace Alliance, said, 'women are powerful beyond measure'.[38] When we really believe that, we can change the world. Governments and development agencies around the world have recognized the power of women in recent years. The Nike Foundation's Girl Effect campaign highlighted the amazing difference girls can make in their communities. Around the world, fewer women work than men and, when they do, they earn less. But when these women and girls do earn money, they reinvest 90 per cent of it into the health, nutrition and educational needs of their families – that's compared to between 30 and 40 per cent for men. In 2006, the Organization for Economic Cooperation and Development measured the economic and political power of women in 162 countries and found that the more power women had, the better the country's economy.

Despite the power we possess, so many of us suffer from low self-esteem. We often see our bodies and ourselves as bad, flawed, imperfect, unworthy, unlovable, un-beautiful. And the effect of that is a lack of confidence. Women with these views of themselves are more likely to think they *can't* than they *can*. And because the world's view of women is that we are more likely to see ourselves in this way, it becomes a self-fulfilling prophecy. Susan Nolen-Hoeksema, author of *The Power of Women*, wrote: 'The perception that women have weak identities and low self-esteem also can discourage the public from believing that women are fit for positions of leadership and power.'[39]

The other half of humanity is not confident in our ability to be world-changers because they see us as frail and insecure, constantly asking whether we are beautiful or not, and crumpling up into a heap when the answer is no. It is true that so often we *are* slaves to beauty. But we don't need to win a beauty pageant to be made free. We are already free indeed. But our salvation has not happened just so that we can feel good about ourselves. You only need to look outside your window to see that the world is broken. Christ followers – each and every one of us – are called to be peace-makers, to be those who make things whole. We are supposed to be world-changers.

The Radiance of Beauty

Mother Teresa was a beautiful woman and a world-changer. You might not think of her as typically beautiful; her wrinkles were signs of her long life of servanthood. She would never have made it on to the front cover of *Vogue* or *Cover Girl*. Yet she radiated the goodness and glory of the God to whom she devoted her life and so in her presence, people saw the beauty of God. Malcolm Muggeridge once described scenes of people watching her during a talk: 'I was watching the faces of people – ordinary people listening to her. Every face, young and old, simple and sophisticated, was rapt with attention, hanging on her words – not because of the words themselves which were quite ordinary, because of her. Some quality came across over and above the words. A luminosity seemed to fill the hall, penetrating every heart and mind.'[40]

Mother Teresa was goodness personified. Her selfless work, ministering to and caring for people the world so often forgets, is the reason she won the Nobel Peace Prize and topped many 'most admired' polls during and after her lifetime. She is one of the greatest examples of inner beauty. I went back to the list in chapter 3, in which I'd asked people to define inner beauty: 'someone with a heart you would love to have', 'a person who shows love and goodness towards all humankind and radiates outwards'. These are fitting descriptions of this amazing woman, who, because of the beauty within her, drew so many people towards the light she emitted. But what spurred her on were neither these accolades, nor a desire to be seen as possessing that inner beauty. Instead, her primary motivation was a desire to fulfil Jesus' commandment to love her neighbour. Speaking at the fourth World Conference on Women in Beijing in 1995, she said:

I often say to people who tell me they would like to serve the poor as I do, 'What I can do, you cannot. What you can do, I cannot. But together we can do something beautiful for God' . . . God told us, 'Love your neighbour as yourself.' So first I am to love myself rightly, and then to love my neighbour like that. But how can I love myself unless I accept myself as God has made me?

Jesus is serious when he commands us to love our neighbours as ourselves in Matthew 22:37–39. There's no greater commandment than loving God first, he says, and then your neighbour as yourself. But so often when I read or hear this passage, I focus on the neighbour. I'm to go out of my way to love my neighbour; to be kind and accepting and loving, to show my neighbour radical hospitality by reflecting a God who loves my neighbour so much. But I tend to skip over the 'as yourself'. It seems a given, that I would love myself, right? But when I look in the mirror in disgust, I am not loving myself. When I wish that I looked like somebody else, I am not loving myself. When thoughts enter my mind about not being beautiful – inside or out – of not being valuable,

> The greatest commandment is not designed just to boost my self-esteem and self-love.

not measuring up or not being good enough, I am not loving myself. I wouldn't dare treat my neighbour the way I have treated myself at times. And what's more, if I am going to see the needs of my neighbour, I cannot be preoccupied with myself anyway. I can't be wrapped up in these feelings of unworthiness. It's only through truly accepting God's love for me – beautiful, just as I am – and realizing that God loves others just as much as he loves me, no matter what stage of life they are at, that I can be freed to change the world.

But in the end, none of this is really about me.

The greatest commandment is not designed just to boost my self-esteem and self-love. It's not really even about my neighbour. It all comes back to loving God. That is the greatest commandment. Everything else follows on from that. He loves us, yes. He thinks we're precious, yes. He thinks we're beautiful, yes. But this love is a two-way thing. He doesn't want us to just keep receiving his love, revelling in it, basking in it and feeling beautiful in it. He wants us – he commands us – to love him with all our heart, with all our soul and with all our mind. Wholly and completely; so that we are totally immersed in loving him. That means every inch of me, all the hidden parts of my heart, all the unknown places in my soul, is to love God in total abandon.

I am beautiful because I am made in his image and am loved by him, my creator. But I love God because he is so utterly beautiful. My beauty is but a pale reflection of his dazzling, stupendous, blinding beauty. I can't help but love him.

There's one thing I ask of God; here's what I want. I want to be where he is forever; every day of my life. Each step along the road of this thing called life, I want to be where he is – in his house. I want to spend eternity looking at just how beautiful he is; how radiant, how stunning, how gorgeous. I want to look for him and find him wherever he is. For he is light and goodness and grace and holiness and beauty itself. There's nothing more I want. There's nothing more I'm looking for.[41]

Acknowledgements

To the friends who talked through ideas with me and shared their own deeply personal thoughts on beauty, thank you. To the virtual friends who told me their stories online, thank you. To Amy for believing in me and pushing me to write from my heart, for Steve at Authentic for taking a chance on me, and Claire for her editing, thank you. To my sisters Chizzie and Ijeoma and my parents Chima and Stella for encouraging me to be all that I can be, thank you.

To my goddaughter Skye – may you grow up in a world that never makes you question your beauty.

And to Beauty himself. Thank you.

Endnotes

All efforts have been made to identify and contact the copyright holders of material reproduced in this work. The author and publisher apologize for any omissions or errors and, if notified, will be pleased to rectify them at the earliest opportunity.

1 'Mirror, mirror', Social Issues Research Centre (SIRC), (1997) http://www.sirc.org/publik/mirror.html
2 *Psychologies Magazine*, February 2013.
3 Arianna Walker, *Mirror Image: Breaking Free From False Reflections* (Presence Books, 2011).
4 'Mirror, mirror', Social Issues Research Centre (SIRC), (1997) http://www.sirc.org/publik/mirror.html
5 American Society of Plastic Surgeons, 2012.
6 http://www.huffingtonpost.com/2012/10/18/hunter-syndrome-hunter-in-focus-positive-exposure_n_1971717.html
7 PGAV destinations http://www.pgavdestinations.com/images/insights/eDestinology_-_Millenials.pdf
8 Desiring God blog http://www.desiringgod.org/resource-library/sermons/jesus-is-precious-because-we-yearn-for-beauty © 1982 John Piper. Used by permission.
9 Katie Piper, *Beautiful*, (Ebury Press, 2011).
10 Dion, Berscheid and Walster, 'What is beautiful is good' in *Journal of Personality & Social Psychology* 24:285–90 (1972).
11 http://www.time.com/time/health/article/0,8599,1906642,00.html
12 Nicolas of Cusa, *The Vision of God*, published by Cosimo (2007), originally published in 1453.

[13] E. *John Walford*, 'The Case for a Broken Beauty' in *The Beauty of God: Theology & the Arts* edited by Treier, Husbands & Lundin (Downers Grove, IVP Academic). Copyright © 2007 by Daniel J. Treier, Mark Husbands and Roger Lundin. Used by permission of InterVarsity Press, PO Box 1400, Downers Grove, IL 60515. www.ivpress.com

[14] Derek and Dianne Tidball, *The Message of Women*, (IVP, 2012).

[15] http://www.youbeauty.com/hair/psychology-of-hair

[16] Anorexia nervosa among female secondary school students in Ghana http://bjp. rcpsych.org/content/185/4/312.short

[17] http://www.hscic.gov.uk/article/2239/Eating-disorder-hospital-admissions-rise-by-16-per-cent-in-a-year

[18] Monica H. Swan PhD et al, 'Perceived Overweight, BMI, and Risk for Suicide Attempts: Findings from the 2007 Youth Risk Behavior Survey', *Journal of Adolescent Health* (June 2009) http://www.jahonline.org/article/S1054-139X(09) 00113-X/ abstract

[19] Amy Frykholm, *See Me Naked: Stories of Sexual Exile in American Christianity* (Beacon Press, 2011).

[20] http://counselingoutfitters.com/vistas/ACAPCD/ACAPCD-35.pdf

[21] www.beautyfromashes.co.uk

[22] Derek and Dianne Tidball, *The Message of Women* (IVP, 2012).

[23] Brené Brown, *The Gifts of Imperfection: Let Go of Who You Think You're Supposed To Be and Embrace Who You Are* (Hazelden Information & Educational Services, 2010).

[24] http://www.dailymail.co.uk/femail/article-2026001/Self-help-books-ruin-life-They-promise-sell-millions.html

[25] *Eating disorders: body image and advertising.* (2000). Retrieved from http://www. healthyplace.com/eating-disorders/main/eating-disorders-body-image-and-advertising/menu-id-58/

[26] Germaine Greer, *The Whole Woman* (Black Swan, 2007).

[27] Blog by Barry Cooper in *The Gospel Coalition* (February 2013) http://thegospelcoalition.org/blogs/tgc/2013/02/25/more-choices-less-commitment/

[28] As quoted in Rachel Held Evans' book *A Year of Biblical Womanhood* (Nashville: Nelson, 2012): Mark Driscoll, The Biblical Admonition to Women to Perform Oral Sex, Christian Research Network, July 2 2009, http://christianresearchnetwork.com/2009/07/02/mark-driscoll-the-biblical-admonition-to-women-to-perform-oral-sex/. (The article has since been taken off the site.)

[29] 'Feminine Protection: The effects of menstruation on attitudes toward women', published in *Psychology of Women Quarterly*, 26, 131–9.

[30] © Tina Beattie, 2002, *God's Mother, Eve's Advocate* Continuum, an imprint of Bloomsbury Publishing Plc.

31 Brené Brown, *The Gifts of Imperfection: Let Go of Who You Think You're Supposed To Be and Embrace Who You Are* (Hazelden Information & Educational Services, 2010).

32 http://www.mothersmovement.org/features/body_image/b_brown_body_shame.htm

33 Philip Yancey, *What's So Amazing About Grace?* (Zondervan, 2002).

34 http://www.worldhealth.net/news/global_anti-aging_products_market_to_rea/

35 http://www.makeupandbeautyblog.com/beauty-tips/how-to-look-great-during-childbirth/

36 http://www.lastmomonearth.com/2012/03/i-am-beautiful-girls.html

37 I first wrote this for Renee Fisher's 'I love my body' series on her blog Devotional Diva www.devotionaldiva.com

38 Marianne Williamson, *A Return to Love: Reflections on the Principles of a Course in Miracles* (Thorsons, 1996).

39 http://www.psychologytoday.com/blog/the-power-women/201001/the-truth-about-women-and-self-esteem

40 Malcolm Muggeridge, *Something Beautiful for God* (Harper & Row, 1971).

41 Adapted from Psalm 27:4.

Be – Godly Wisdom to Live By

365 devotions for women

Fiona Castle and friends

Jesus gave us the greatest love of all. We are called not just to keep it to ourselves, but to overflow with that love to others. But how can we really do that in the busyness of our lives?

In these daily devotions, women from many walks of life share insights on scripture and practical life lessons to gently encourage you to live for Jesus, and to be more like him in your thoughts, character, and actions.

Discover godly wisdom that will help you navigate the world as a Christian woman and live out God's unique purpose for your life.

978-1-78893-239-4

Authentic

We trust you enjoyed reading this book
from Authentic. If you want to be
informed of any new titles from this author
and other releases you can sign up to the
Authentic newsletter by scanning below:

Online:
authenticmedia.co.uk

Follow us: